Canada's Road

Mark Richardson

CANADA'S ROAD

A Journey on the
Trans-Canada Highway
from St. John's to Victoria

DUNDURN
TORONTO

Editor: Cheryl Hawley
Design: Courtney Horner
Printer: Webcom

Library and Archives Canada Cataloguing in Publication

Richardson, Mark, 1962-
    Canada's road : a journey on the Trans-Canada Highway from
St. John's to Victoria / Mark Richardson.

Issued also in electronic formats.
ISBN 978-1-4597-0979-9

1   2   3   4   5   17   16   15   14   13

We acknowledge the support of the **Canada Council for the Arts** and the **Ontario Arts Council** for our publishing program. We also acknowledge the financial support of the **Government of Canada** through the **Canada Book Fund** and **Livres Canada Books**, and the **Government of Ontario** through the **Ontario Book Publishing Tax Credit** and the **Ontario Media Development Corporation**.

Care has been taken to trace the ownership of copyright material used in this book. The author and the publisher welcome any information enabling them to rectify any references or credits in subsequent editions.

J. Kirk Howard, President

Printed and bound in Canada.

Visit us at
Dundurn.com
Definingcanada.ca
@dundurnpress
Facebook.com/dundurnpress

Dundurn	Gazelle Book Services Limited	Dundurn
3 Church Street, Suite 500	White Cross Mills	2250 Military Road
Toronto, Ontario, Canada	High Town, Lancaster, England	Tonawanda, NY
M5E 1M2	LA1 4XS	U.S.A. 14150

For Albert Todd and Perry Doolittle,
who would have loved to drive the Trans-Canada Highway

ST. JOHN'S, NL — I'm at the eastern start of the Trans-Canada Highway, preparing for an 8,000-kilometre drive west along the highway to the other end in Victoria, BC, which also thinks of itself as the start of the road.

In Victoria there's a large sign in a park beside the road down by the Pacific that declares itself "Mile Zero." There's no such sign here. There is a sports complex downtown called the Mile One Centre, but it's not technically on the highway.

No — the TCH begins in Atlantic Canada at the dump.

"The TCH technically begins on the Outer Ring Road at the Logy Bay Road overpass," says Emily Timmins, the communications manager for Newfoundland's Department of Transportation and Works. That's about five kilometres from downtown. If you drive in from the west, as I did, then the road just keeps going without anything to suggest you're no longer on the TCH until you pass the Robin Hood Bay Regional Waste Management Facility and, after a kilometre or so, come to a stop at Quidi Vidi Lake.

It was not an auspicious end to the 4,000 kilometres I'd just driven from Toronto, so I headed over to the Mile One Centre for a photo. Tom Petty was playing that night and parking was an issue; security tried to shoo me from putting the car right beside the sign, but a gentle chat and a little persuasion won the day.

I'll be telling stories as I drive west. Two thousand twelve is not just the 50th anniversary of the Trans-Canada Highway opening officially in 1962, on the day I was born, but also the 100th anniversary of the first road trip through Canada from ocean to ocean.

There were several pioneering drives across the country before it became simple, and I'll also be retracing their routes and telling their stories:

- The Thomas Wilby drive of 1912, in which a snooty English journalist was chauffeured across the country and wrote a book that never once named his driver.
- The Perry Doolittle drive of 1925, in which the founder of the Canadian Automobile Association swapped the wheels of his Model-T Ford to drive along railway tracks where there were no roads.
- The Alex Macfarlane drive of 1946, the first time anybody was able to drive across the country on all-Canadian roads. That trip earned Macfarlane the Todd Medal, created in 1912 by the future mayor of Victoria to award to the first person to drive across Canada, all four wheels on the road.

I'm carrying the Todd Medal with me on this road trip. I'm also carrying a horseshoe from Wilby's journey and a 1925 CAA radiator badge. I'll be more comfortable than all those pioneers, of course. General Motors provided me with a 2012 Chevy Camaro convertible for this drive, and the CAA is ready to rescue me should I get into any trouble. That may happen when I dip the wheels of the Camaro into the ocean here to begin the journey — I'm hoping the wharf won't be too slippery, and this journey doesn't end in the water before it's even begun....

Follow me on this road trip, and we'll explore Canada together.

Day 1: Trinity Bay, NL
Trans-Canada Distance: 90 kilometres

THEN: (Whitbourne) It's not been so far to drive today, but back in 1962 this was the end of the paved road west from St. John's. The highway turned to corrugated gravel before Whitbourne and separated the casual tourists from the determined traveller.

Author Edward McCourt described his 1963 drive along it, in his book *The Road Across Canada*, as "an endless succession of iron-surfaced washboard, gaping pot-holes, and naked rock — a shoulder-twisting, neck-snapping, dust-shrouded horror." And by all other accounts, he was being kind.

It was not until 1965, when McCourt's book was published, that the road was properly paved across the province, at great expense. And canny premier Joey Smallwood made sure the great expense came from the pockets of the federal government, not the provincial coffers.

Edward McCourt.

NOW: (Petty Harbour) I began my drive with the Camaro's wheels in the Atlantic Ocean, dipping into the water on a wharf at Petty Harbour, just south of Cape Spear, the most easterly point in Canada. Like all the pioneering drivers, it's important to drive out of one ocean in order to drive eventually into the other one at the opposite side of the country. I did a trial run with some friends yesterday, but then it was late in the afternoon and today it was noon: low tide.

The reluctant tide meant I had to drive a lot farther down the boat ramp, with the rear driving wheels venturing down onto the wet concrete that had been submerged just a couple of hours earlier. It was very slippery. The CBC sent a cameraman to record the event for posterity, and he slid his shoes around on the concrete. "If this is too slippery for those tires, this video could go viral," he warned, probably rather hopefully. Last year a YouTube video of a million-dollar Ferrari Enzo crashing into the sea during the Targa Newfoundland was viewed millions of times. You can see it online if you have a cruel sense of humour — and irony.

The Camaro dips its wheels in the Atlantic.

But all went well, the wide tires gripped and the car made it back onto the road. I gathered some salty Atlantic water in a bottle, which I'll pour into the salty Pacific when I reach the opposite coast, and then drove into St. John's with the top down for a last look at the Mile One Centre before heading out to the dump and the real start of the Trans-Canada Highway.

SOMETHING DIFFERENT: (Dildo) The towns have colourful names in Newfoundland. Here's local businessman Kevin Nolan, the owner of the

Mark Richardson

Captain Dildo, the town mascot of Dildo, NL.

nearby Dildo Dory Grill, describing the communities of Trinity Bay: "You turn just before you get to Come-By-Chance, you go past Spreadeagle, and then you get to Dildo. After you leave Dildo, you enter Shag Rock, and then it's Heart's Delight and then Heart's Desire and Heart's Content. And then you enter Conception Bay. That's just before Cupids."

He took a photo of me with a statue of the town's mascot, Captain Dildo, named for the town which is supposedly named after a place in Spain — nobody's really sure. The statue is cemented into the ground, to stop it suffering the same fate as the road signs whenever college students come to visit.

Day 2: Gambo, NL
Trans-Canada Distance: 301 kilometres

THEN: (Gambo) Every Newfoundlander knows where Gambo is, because every Newfoundlander knows that this is where Joey Smallwood was born — the man who became the first Newfoundland premier when he signed his province into Confederation in 1949, and the man who mastered the art of wringing dollars out of Ottawa.

The Trans-Canada Highway was no exception. In 1962, when the TCH was declared officially open by Prime Minister John Diefenbaker, 600 kilometres of its 980-kilometre stretch across The Rock was still unpaved; when the circus wanted to come to town in 1963 it ended up cancelling because highway bridges wouldn't support the weight of the elephants, which would have had to be walked separately from their trucks over the road's numerous river crossings.

The agreement first proposed in 1949 between Ottawa and the provinces called for each province to share the cost of construction 50/50 with the federal government, though Ottawa would pay the cost of road-building through national parks. Smallwood delayed construction while he spent his provincial money on other things, like schools and hospitals. In 1964 he argued that hardscrabble Newfoundland just couldn't afford to complete the highway, and eventually Lester Pearson's new Liberal government caved and agreed to foot 90 percent of the bill. "That'll do nicely," said Smallwood, and promptly coined a provincial slogan: "We'll finish the drive in '65." Which they did on November 27, 1965, when the last strip of asphalt was laid and two convoys of cars, one from St. John's with Smallwood among them, and one from Port aux Basques that included Pearson, met halfway across the province in Grand Falls.

I'm headed to Grand Falls tomorrow. I'll go look at Pearson's Peak — the monument erected to thank the prime minister for cutting the big cheque.

NOW: (Clarenville) I noticed the bicycles propped against the window of the Tim Hortons when I walked inside. They looked heavy, loaded with luggage. Another bicycle was propped against the other door and it looked even heavier. The cyclists were inside, greeting each other as they met for the first time, cycling in opposite directions across the country..

Will Samson-Doel, Harry Jones, Daman Milsom, and Kibby Evans.

Daman Milsom and Kibby Evans, both recently graduated biology students, are cycling home to Victoria. They flew in to St. John's last week and left Cape Spear four days ago, pedalling into the west wind.

Harry Jones and Will Samson-Doel, both university students with a summer to themselves, left home in Toronto on May 1 and expect to reach St. John's by Friday. Then they'll fly with their bikes to Vancouver and cycle home from there.

All are in their early 20s and none of them have done any serious cycling before these journeys. Daman and Kibby had never ridden farther than 60 kilometres in a day, and Harry and Will were even less prepared: "I only used a bicycle to commute," said Will, "and I've never commuted more than 15 minutes. You don't need to be super-athletic to do this. You just need the time, and the bike."

The Toronto cyclists had seen only one other pair of cyclists before today, in Nova Scotia, and they'd not stopped to chat while they pedalled in different directions. Are they having fun? "Yes, in most ways, this is what we expected," said Harry. "Once you're into the rhythm and your legs have adjusted, it's a great way to travel." His friend Will agreed: "I've never been east of Quebec City. I didn't expect to see such differences between the provinces."

The greenhorn Westerners were pleased to hear this, since they've cycled only a little more than 200 kilometres so far and the weather's been terrible. "I've been surprised by the weather," said Kibby. "I thought uphills would be bad, but the downhills — you go so fast and the wind's so cold. At least uphill you get warmer with the pedalling."

All four are doing their cross-Canada rides to raise money and awareness for causes close to their hearts. Harry and Will say they've raised $13,000 so far for the First Nations Child and Family Caring Society; you can read their blog at *willandharrybikecanada.blogspot.ca*. Daman and Kibby say they've raised $16,000 toward a $50,000 goal for Trekking4Transplants, which also hopes to persuade 10,000 people to become organ donors. You can read about them on their website at *trekking4transplants.ca*.

I wished them well, got in the Camaro, and turned up the heat as I drove west. I didn't want my coffee getting cold.

Mark Richardson

Mark with Newfoundland's first premier.

SOMETHING DIFFERENT: (Gambo) Here in former-premier Joey Smallwood's hometown, the man seems honoured with the same level of reverence that North Koreans offer their late Dear Leaders.

The scenic lookout beside the TCH above town, with its dramatic view over Freshwater Bay, is named after Smallwood, but there's little evidence that he would come to ponder the vista. However, a massive black-and-white photograph of his head looks out from here now that he's been dead these last 20 years.

Newfoundlanders may hold Smallwood dear in their thoughts, but, in their words, they're far more practical. Us Mainlanders call the site "Joey's Lookout," but it's known across the island as "The Big Giant Head."

Day 3: Grand Falls, NL
Trans-Canada Distance: 441 kilometres

THEN: (Grand Falls) When Premier Joey Smallwood drove west from St. John's in 1965 to greet Prime Minister Lester B. Pearson, who was driving east from Port aux Basques, they met just outside town here at the provincial halfway point of the fully paved Trans-Canada Highway. In doing so, the TCH was declared complete across Newfoundland. "We finished this drive in '65," declared the signs and posters, "thanks to Mr. Pearson."

As I recounted yesterday, Pearson agreed to pay 90 percent of the cost of the road's construction in order to get it finished while he was in office, and the province set to with vigour while Smallwood knew the funds were available. In appreciation, a monument was erected at the halfway point — a rock pillar roughly 25 metres high — and it was named "Pearson's Peak" to commemorate the federal generosity.

But there's nothing there now. Nobody here is quite sure what became of it. Long-time residents recall that it fell into disrepair after the two back-slapping Liberals left office; it became unsafe, with pieces of rock sometimes falling from it near the cars that were parked by amorous couples. There was nothing else to do there, after all — no picnic area or green space, just a circle of asphalt surrounded by bush with a pillar in the middle, about 100 metres up from the road.

The province chose the cheaper option of dismantling it instead of repairing it; again, nobody in town is quite sure when, though the tourism people in St. John's say it was removed in 1997. The entrance to the paved drive was dug up to prevent cars from going in, and aside from some rubble and firewood sticks, there's nothing whatsoever to mark the spot.

What happened to the bronze sign on the peak? Apparently it was found at a landfill site, but where it went then no one can — or will — say.

NOW: (Norris Arm) There are signs all along the highway in Newfoundland warning of moose on the road. I can't recall seeing a single one, despite driving through both national parks and covering more than 2,000 kilometres on the island, both east and west.

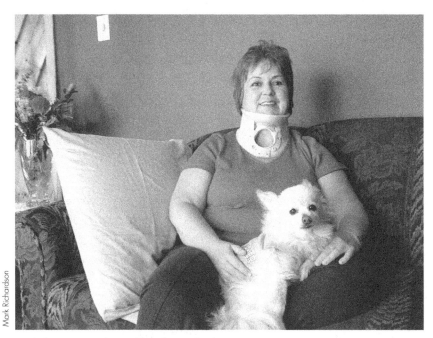

Mark Richardson

Michelle Higgins with DJ, who's a lot smaller than a moose.

Michelle Higgins also doesn't recall seeing a moose recently, though she surely did early last month when she was driving in the evening from her home at Norris Arm to work at Gander. I dropped in to see her this morning, so let her tell the story:

"I remember looking at the clock and I seen 7:28. The police officer said after that must have been the time that I hit the moose. The next thing I know, I was pulling into work's driveway. I remember getting out of the car, and I remember my co-worker coming up and putting her arm around me, and asked me if I was OK, and I kind of looked at her and asked her, 'Well, why wouldn't I be?' And she said, 'Michelle, you're bleeding.' She said, 'Look at your car — were you in an accident?' I said, 'No, I wasn't in an accident.' And she said, 'Did you hit a moose?' I said, 'No, I never even seen a moose, let alone hit one.' She said, 'Look at your car,' and when I turned around and looked at my car, I couldn't believe it."

The windshield was smashed in and the roof peeled back "like a sardine tin." Higgins is now famous as the woman who drove more than 30 kilometres along the TCH in an open, wrecked car, with no recollection whatsoever of hitting the moose that police found dead on the road.

She's lost count of the journalists who've found her on the phone in Norris Arm; she's not in the directory, though there are plenty of Higgins who all know each other. New York, Chicago, London — they've all been calling. "My cousin is in South Africa, and she saw it in the paper there," she says. They're all intrigued that she would have kept driving, and by all accounts of the few people who noticed her, driving quite responsibly.

She's off work now from her job as a behavioural therapist because two of the bones in her neck are broken and she must wear a brace to help them heal. As well, she cannot lie flat without becoming nauseous, and she's booked for a third MRI in a couple of weeks to check her progress. The accident hasn't stopped her from being driven on the Trans-Canada, though.

"The first time I drove out there, I had knots and butterflies in my stomach, thinking that it would all come back to me, but I didn't remember a thing," she says. "Maybe it's good that I don't remember. I've seen maybe 10 moose in 10 years, on the road, and then I went to St. John's the other day with my son and on the way back, we saw three moose. I wasn't worried."

SOMETHING DIFFERENT: (Grand Falls) It's been raining all day. ALL DAY! I haven't seen the sun in more than a week. And it's cold: seven degrees at most. So much for driving a convertible.

There's no point griping about this to Newfoundlanders though. "Aye, it's some terrible ting, but dat's de way she is," said my host this morning. They're calling it "Juneuary." Apparently, last June it rained 23 days of the month. People here are hoping this summer will be better and are quick to say that April and May were warm and pleasant months. And the weather is good right now in Labrador, apparently.

Day 4: Port aux Basques, NL
Trans-Canada Distance: 921 kilometres

THEN: (Whitbourne) Lloyd Adams is "on the light side of 77," and when I met him, he and his wife, Audrey, were celebrating their 48th wedding anniversary. But before they married, Lloyd spent years in the bush, surveying the future Trans-Canada Highway across Newfoundland.

"I got the job straight from school and stayed for 13, 14 years," he said. "I learned everything on the job. Started as an engineer's assistant, holding the tape, then worked my way up to using the instruments and plotting the road. We took it for granted back then and it was just a job, dealing with the blackflies, drinking water out of a boghole." He paused, and then he said, "We didn't realize it at the time, but we really were pioneers."

There was no complete road across Newfoundland when he began in the mid-50s. From Clarenville to Gambo, cars had to be carried by

Lloyd and Audrey Adams.

Mark Richardson

train, on the rail-car ferry. Lloyd would trek into the bush with a team of half-a-dozen surveyors for weeks at a time, hauling their own supplies and building their own camps. When they'd surveyed five kilometres of potential road, they'd pull up the camp and move it the five kilometres to the start of the next leg and begin again.

At least they had their own cook, and he didn't have to do the heavy work — the clearing of the survey lines was done by another team of six men, equipped only with axes.

"It was tough land to work on," he remembered. "You'd get to a pond and the construction crew would have to drain it and fill it all in, or to a rock and have to blow through it. These days, you don't even notice when you're speeding past.

"Now we have a four-lane highway and it only takes 45 minutes to get to Walmart. I guess that's progress."

NOW: (Corner Brook) There's one word that describes today: Monsoon.

The drive from Grand Falls was just a slog along a soaking wet, spray-filled road. Any scenery worth seeing was hidden behind a wall of water, or of cloud, until I got to the west coast. The Trans-Canada Highway here is a slippery road, too. More often than not there were two channels of rainwater where the asphalt has been depressed into shallow tracks by years of vehicles driving the same point in the lane.

Where there was standing water, which was frequent, the wide and sporty tires of the Camaro slid from side to side, jerking the car. Wider tires mean there's less weight concentrated on the same area of rubber than regular tires, which does not make for a relaxing drive. I don't really want to be calling the CAA for a tow truck out of the ditch in my first week on the road — give me moose any day.

SOMETHING DIFFERENT: (South Branch) How do you market the unmarketable? Somebody at Gale's Septic Pumping north of Port aux Basques found a way.

With a captive audience driving past all day long, these 1,000-gallon septic tanks are lined up beside the road to greet drivers.

Mark Richardson

Yes, they really are septic tanks.

And no, I didn't check if they were empty.

Day 5: Rose Blanche, NL
Trans-Canada Distance: 921 kilometres

THEN: (Rose Blanche) You get to Rose Blanche by turning right instead of left when you leave the ferry at Port aux Basques, or by carrying on an extra 42 kilometres when you get to the western end of the paved Trans-Canada Highway in Newfoundland.

That's what author Edward McCourt did when he drove the TCH in 1963. The ferry was fully booked, so he and his wife Margaret were forced to spend an extra day on The Rock. Here's what he had to say in his book, *The Road Across Canada,*

The thirty mile run by car from Port aux Basques to

Rose Blanche at the end of the road is one of the most novel and spectacular in all Newfoundland. The road, a new one, is surprisingly good and safe considering that much of it appears blasted out of solid rock....

Rose Blanche more than fulfills our dreams of what a Newfoundland village ought to look like.... Houses perch on the point and the off-shore rocks and cling to the cliff faces rising from the water's edge. The parts of the village are bound together by elevated wooden sidewalks snaking over water and rock and occasionally a substance that might pass for land. Since most places in the village are accessible mostly by boat, Rose Blanche suggests a Venice in miniature — if you can accept a fish-packing plant for a doge's palace and a rowboat for a gondola.

The wooden sidewalks are gone, but not much else has changed.

Rose Blanche today.

Mark Richardson

NOW: (Petites) I stayed here last week on my first night in Newfoundland, after reading McCourt's description, and met Lynne Sawford and Norm Gentner, a couple from Petawawa, Ontario, who run the excellent Rose Sea Guest House in town. Just as well, it's the only place in town to stay and it's one of those hidden secrets of the province. They took me for a walk to the granite lighthouse that is the community's only tourist attraction, and pointed out the tiny community of Petites across the bay, about three kilometres east of here and past the end of the road.

I was intrigued by the distant houses, empty now since the government resettled the place in 2003 and forced its residents to move. Lynne arranged for a boat to take me out there for a poke around on my return, which was today.

I swallowed a Gravol, got into the small boat, and held on gamely to my life preserver; men here usually refuse to wear them on the water, despite very few knowing how to swim.

It took 20 minutes to get across the bay and I was dropped at the

Mark Richardson

Austin Bennett, left, and Wayne Spencer.

old wharf. Petites used to be a community of a couple of dozen houses, complete with church, school, and fire hall, but the buildings have fallen apart in the last nine years they've been empty. I walked through a number of them over the next couple of hours, shooting video and saying wistful things into the microphone, until I walked down an overgrown path and heard voices.

It was Austin Bennett chatting with his lobsterman friend Wayne Spencer. Bennett was born and raised at Petites and never really left. "I was the last one to sign the papers," he told me, sitting on the porch of the house he still owns. "I took the money the government gave me and bought a place in Rose Blanche. The family's there, but I still come here to lobster fish in the summer."

It's like a cabin in the woods, he said, except that it's on the ocean and accessed only by boat. His Petites home has a generator and a wood-burning stove, and inside it looks like any other cottage. A couple of other people have also maintained houses in the settlement and come to stay every summer.

Mmmm — whole squid, maybe? Or cod cheeks?

"There's nothing to stop me being here, so why would I leave?" he reasoned. It's a base for lobster fishing, and a getaway when the hectic pace of Rose Blanche, population 600, grows too much for him. Is he nostalgic for the old community?

Not really, he says. There's no fishing anymore, except for the lobster that he takes from around the harbour, and most of the community had already moved away by 2003 to find work elsewhere — maybe a dozen people were left.

Back in Rose Blanche, I tell Norm and Lynne about my bittersweet afternoon at Petites, and I ask them if they think their adopted town will ever be abandoned. They're both sure it will. Already, most of the men work in Alberta, and the women also work elsewhere.

"I don't know if this will last 30 years," says Norm, and then Lynne cuts in: "But we're going to make the most of it while we can — while it's still here. It's too wonderful to leave."

SOMETHING DIFFERENT: (Port aux Basques) In Newfoundland little goes to waste, and that includes food. I stopped at a Port aux Basques fish shop that leaves out nothing that could possibly be eaten — including cod and halibut cheeks, whole squid, and squid tubes — though not by me.

Days 6/7: Baddeck, NS
Trans-Canada Distance: 979 kilometres

THEN: (Louisbourg) In 1946, Brigadier R.A. (Alex) Macfarlane (retired) and his friend Ken MacGillivray, a former RCAF squadron leader, drove their new Chevrolet Stylemaster, borrowed from General Motors, to Louisburg, NS, and dipped its wheels in the Atlantic there. Then they set off for the Pacific to become the first drivers to cross the country entirely on Canadian roads.

Brigadier R.A. (Alex) Macfarlane.

For doing so they were awarded the Todd Medal, struck in 1912 by Albert Todd, who would later become mayor of Victoria, BC. The medal was created to promote automobile use and adventure, and to encourage the connection of Canadian communities to each other by road, instead of just to their markets in the U.S.

Back in 1912, Todd expected that his gold medal would be awarded within five years or so, but it took until 1943 for the final stretch of gravel highway to be completed between Geraldton and Hearst in northern Ontario before it was possible to drive across Canada by road. Even then it was an ordeal, made more difficult by wartime gas rationing, and it took another three years before Macfarlane learned of the medal's existence and set out on his epic drive.

In the end it took just 13 days to make the drive from Louisburg, then the most easterly point in Canada (Newfoundland would not join confederation for another three years) to Victoria, with a day's layover in Winnipeg.

They ran into snow in northern Ontario, and some hairpin turns in British Columbia "gave us several thrills," reported Macfarlane. He called the road trip "gruelling," but they experienced only two flat tires on the mostly unpaved highways and averaged almost 800 kilometres a day.

The medal was awarded to Macfarlane in Victoria, but not by Todd. The mayor had died in office 18 years previously.

Mark Richardson

The Todd Medal (front).

Mark Richardson

The Todd Medal (reverse).

On its back, the medal names Macfarlane as "First Motorist to drive Auto Across Canada on all Canadian Highways." MacGillivray was not mentioned because he did not drive the car and was considered only an observer.

I have the Todd Medal with me now, carrying it securely in the car, on loan from Macfarlane's grandson Jim. So today I drove up from Baddeck on a sidetrip to Louisburg, the site of the former French fortress of the 18th century. The fortress was not yet restored in 1946, but no matter — because the tourist season does not begin until next week I was able to drive right up to the site and pose for a photo in front of the main building. Then I got into the 2012 Chevrolet Camaro convertible, borrowed from General Motors, and set off again for the Pacific.

NOW: (New Harris Forks) I crossed on the ferry yesterday to Nova Scotia and drove down to Baddeck. Along the way the highway crosses the graceful Seal Island Bridge to climb up and over Kelly's Mountain. A sign at the bottom warns that the road rises 240 metres in the next seven kilometres.

Part of the original standard for the Trans-Canada Highway calls for drivers to always be able to see 600 feet (200 metres) ahead of their vehicle, but this is clearly not possible at the curve in the road at the northern end of the mountain, which has a recommended speed limit of 40 kilometres per hour. Forward visibility there is perhaps 100 metres. There have been numerous fatal crashes on this mountain thanks to this sharp curve.

Local lore tells that the highway could easily have crossed the water 20 kilometres south, where a ferry used to operate, which would have avoided the mountain entirely, but a local politician pressed for the current route in order to benefit from profitable land sales to the government.

Fifty years later and the road still contains this dangerous curve, perhaps the sharpest on the highway in the country. I'll see if there's anything similar in British Columbia when I pass through there next month, and get back to this then.

SOMETHING DIFFERENT: (Baddeck) I was going to just take a photo of the Lick-A-Chick Restaurant that's outside North Sydney, and mention that apparently Wayne Gretzky went in there a few years ago and bought up all the hats and T-shirts for his buddies, but a friend convinced me to go with the Maine-iacs instead.

I stopped at Baddeck two weeks ago, on the way east to start this journey in Newfoundland. I'd met up with my brother-in-law and my niece, who were both running in the annual 300-kilometre Cabot Trail Relay, and went with them to the wrap party that afternoon at the Bras d'Or Yacht Club.

Halfway through, the winning team — the Maine-iacs, who are perennial champions from, you guessed it, Maine — stripped off without warning and plunged into the lake to celebrate. Then they had to get out.

There was much cheering and calling from the club's deck. I walked after with some women from Newfoundland who were still recovering from the sight. "Seventeen naked men, all in one place!" said one. "I've never seen so much tackle. I wish I had a photo."

Mark Richardson

The Maine-iacs, cooling off at Baddeck.

Well, here it is. The original is available at no charge to any of the Maine-iacs who would like it — maybe to burn it …

Day 8: Charlottetown, PEI
Trans-Canada Distance: 1,262 kilometres

THEN: (Port Hastings) The causeway that links Cape Breton to the rest of mainland Canada is only a few years older than the Trans-Canada Highway, opened officially in August 1955. Kevin MacDonald remembers being there as an 11-year-old boy, while his mom sold hotdogs to the crowd and his father, a train-ferry engineer at nearby Port Hawkesbury, worried about losing his job.

"I remember the bagpipes," he recalls. "They were loud!"

Mark Richardson

Kevin MacDonald at the Canso Causeway.

Perhaps not quite as loud as they might have been, though. There's a story, which nobody can prove true or false, that says one of the 100 pipers who marched across the Canso Causeway that day refused to actually blow into his pipes — a protest against the perceived loss of his island's independence. He was, apparently, a proud Cape Bretoner named Roderick (Big Rod the Piper) MacPherson, and some people say the story's true while others say it's a misty-eyed fantasy.

Whatever the case, it is true that several hundred people lost their jobs when the causeway was completed and the ferry service ended, including Kevin's dad, but Charles MacDonald's position at CN was transferred to Sydney the following year. Kevin says he and his sister received a better education for it. And in the end, the towns of Port Hawkesbury and Port Hastings saw more industry come to their area from the improved connection, and more jobs.

Does Kevin have a favourite memory of that August day, 57 years ago? Sure he does. "The premier responsible for the causeway, Angus L. MacDonald, had died the year before and so his brother gave a speech for him. His brother was Father Stanley, and he spoke in the traditional Gaelic to the crowd, who all understood the language. And he gave them his opinion of what he really thought of the politicians. The people all laughed and cheered and so the politicians, who were sitting behind Father Stanley, all laughed and cheered too. They weren't from Cape Breton and couldn't understand anything he was saying — just as well too. And that's a true story. There's lots of verification for that one."

NOW: (Pictou) Peter the truck driver parked his haul of gravel among a dozen other gravel trucks in the line to enter the PEI ferry at Pictou, Nova Scotia. "We haul gravel and sand onto the island, and we're taking contaminated soil out," he says. There's really no sand and gravel on Prince Edward Island that's good enough quality to build roads or mix concrete, and it must all be imported from quarries in Nova Scotia. But the contaminated soil — what's that about?

"They found an oil tank was leaking into the ground in Charlottetown and they don't know how much oil is there. Enough to keep us busy anyway. They've dug down eight metres so far and they don't know when they'll stop."

Peter is one of the drivers who take the oily soil to a landfill in Nova Scotia that can process it properly, and their trucks fill the lower level of the ferry. It's expensive to cross, he says — nearly $130 round trip. Vehicles driving to and from PEI only pay when they leave the island, not when they enter, and it's more expensive to use the seasonal ferry than the Confederation Bridge — about $20 more. Because of that, people in the know who need to make a round-trip loop will leave the island on the bridge and return on the ferry.

Like the ferries to Newfoundland, and the BC ferries between Vancouver's Horseshoe Bay and Nanaimo on Vancouver Island, the 22-kilometre crossing of the PEI ferry is considered to be a part of the Trans-Canada Highway. There's been a ferry here since 1937, 20 years after the first regular ferry to the island was established near the current site of the Confederation Bridge.

Today maybe half the 100-or-so passengers are watching Ellen Degeneres on the small ship's large TV. Reception is better than when two friends of mine crossed on their honeymoon to the island, on the morning of September 11, 2001. It was horrible, Simon told me later. Everyone knew something terrible had happened but they really couldn't make it out properly on the news with the snowy reception. When they got to PEI, he said, people heard on their car radios as they disembarked that New York's Twin Towers had been destroyed, and everybody seemed to drive away in shock.

SOMETHING DIFFERENT: (Orwell) They didn't have Camaros in the 1890s — not even the originals. For that matter, they didn't have Jeannie Campbell either, but they did have the character she plays, Mrs. Clarke of the general store. Jeannie is an interpreter at the Orwell Corner Historic Village, just off the Trans-Canada Highway about 30 kilometres east of Charlottetown.

Jeannie took the time at the end of her day today to check out the 2012 car and decided she liked it, though she's going to keep her Honda Civic for now. She says she likes her job, too, and the people she meets every summer, and she's no stranger to having her photo taken.

"We get a lot of Japanese visitors here," she said. They come to see Anne of Green Gables and then they come here, too. "They like this place because it's the same time period [as Anne], and it's real, too. These are the original buildings from the 1890s.

"They all want to take my picture, and I tell them they can take as many as they want, but I don't ever want to see them."

Day 9: Charlottetown, PEI

Trans-Canada Distance: 1,262 kilometres

THEN: (Charlottetown) When the federal government passed an act, in 1949, to "encourage and assist the construction of a trans-Canada highway," it proposed splitting the cost 50/50 with the provinces for the construction of a road that would be built to a uniformly high standard.

Quebec and all the eastern provinces were reluctant to agree, because they would have to spend money to improve existing roads they already considered good enough — with the exception of Prince Edward Island. PEI was pleased to sign right away on the dotted line. It wanted a bridge or a tunnel to connect it to the mainland, and it saw this co-operation as only beneficial toward that.

Of course, it also had by far the least amount of highway to construct: just 120 kilometres between the New Brunswick ferry at Borden and the Nova Scotia ferry at Wood Islands. Its relative costs were higher, though, since all gravel for the base had to be imported from Nova Scotia.

NOW: (Charlottetown) PEI's transport minister runs his finger along a smooth line on the map. "This is the new route the highway will be taking," says Robert Vessey. He doesn't need to waggle his finger along the other line, which twists sharply on the paper and is the current position of the road.

At Churchill it needs realignment, he explains. People don't like change, especially here on the island, and there have been numerous public meetings to determine the new route that the Trans-Canada Highway should take in this area. The realignment has to be done, though — there's a higher accident rate on this stretch than anywhere else on the highway, thanks to the relatively tight turns and steep grades.

"We're trying to avoid expropriation (of private land)," says Vessey. "We're dealing with all the landowners and, so far, we don't have all the deals done, but we're close. We're negotiating — some are tougher than others, but so far we haven't expropriated any land."

The existing road surface needed to be replaced anyway, thanks to the significantly increased heavy truck traffic from when it was first constructed in 1952. That would have cost the province $9 million. But if the Trans-Canada Highway is reconstructed, rather than just maintained, then the 1949 agreement still holds true and Ottawa will pay for half. The 6.1 kilometres of new road is estimated to cost $16 million, which means PEI need pay only half that, saving the province a million dollars and providing a safer highway, too.

SOMETHING DIFFERENT: (New Haven) The 1989 Volkswagen Golf Cabriolet I saw parked beside the road is "a good little car," says owner Scott Dawson, but he's bought a newer model, a 2001, so it's not needed anymore and he put a FOR SALE sign on it. I had to give him a call.

"It's not a car I'll let my children drive," he says. "They'll get somewhere and then some little hiccup will happen with it and it won't start, and I'll have to go get them and fix it. I'm always driving my kids to sports, so I said I might as well drive something fun. I didn't buy it for the roof — I only drive it with the top down."

Scott's asking $4,750, which is about one-tenth the price of the 2012 Chevy Camaro I'm driving, but he says he's open to offers.

Day 10: Borden, PEI
Trans-Canada Distance: 1,317 kilometres

THEN: (Charlottetown) The Trans-Canada Highway used to come right through the middle of Charlottetown, along Grafton Street and up University Avenue. This was common practice across the country in 1962, because merchants wanted the inevitable traffic from tourists.

In Montreal, for example, the Trans-Canada Highway was officially placed right on Ste-Catherine Street downtown. But the merchants also got the inevitable truck traffic that comes with hauling goods around the country, and there are now bypasses to redirect traffic around commercial centres.

The Charlottetown bypass did not begin construction until the early 1980s, but today it loops around the island's capital city. Some 200 trucks use it on average each day, staying well clear of the centre of town.

NOW: (New Haven) At the risk of over-alliteration, Prince Edward Island is an impossibly pretty, postcard-perfect province, and the Trans-Canada Highway dips and winds its way directly through several communities on its way between the bridge and the ferry. This may be pleasant on the two-lane portions, but it's not efficient — and it's dangerous. More accidents occur along the 6.1-kilometre stretch near New Haven than anywhere else, and so, as I wrote in yesterday's blog, the province is widening and straightening that portion of road. Thirty-five properties will no longer have their driveways opening directly onto the TCH.

But not everyone is happy about this. "It doesn't make any sense," says Miller Choi, who owns the Bonshaw Amusement Park. There's a small go-kart track on the 10 acres of land, as well as a pool for bumper boats and a mini-golf course, and it fronts directly onto the Trans-Canada. When the new road goes through on the other side of the trees behind, the amusement park will be cut off completely by the forest and drivers won't see that it exists.

Miller Choi beside his go-kart track.

This was the first go-kart track in PEI and has been there for 42 years, says Choi. He doesn't understand why the road is being directed behind his property and not in front of it, where it would continue to remove the sharp curve at the top of his hill.

"I bought this place (in 2005) for its exposure onto the highway," he says. "In the summer, we get more than a hundred visitors a day, but we'll lose that. It will all be terribly worse, but the government doesn't care."

Choi wants the government to compensate him for lost business, or buy his property at a fair current price, but he's heard nothing from enquiries he's made. And he's not the only person who's affected by the new routing.

"I really don't want to talk about it — everything's in negotiations," says the man who comes to the door of the white house on the other side of the hill. The house was built in 1862, and the new road will go right through its living room. He says he's lived there for 47 years, but he doesn't know where he'll move to when his home is demolished for the road. As for protesting, he says he has no choice — when the government wants to do something, they just do it.

He does acknowledge, though, that the current stretch of road is dangerous. "There's at least two, three, four times a year that people come knocking on my door and say they've put a car in the ditch," he says.

Alex Calder is also losing part of his property's lawn, but he's circumspect about the situation. "I can see the positives in it," he says, pointing out how the new route will flatten the hill and remove two sharp S-curves. "Water drains down the road here and then freezes on the curve, where it's in shadow, and cars, trucks hit the glare ice and that's it for them. It'll be a lot safer when it's done, and that's what's important, isn't it?"

SOMETHING DIFFERENT: (Hunter River) If everything's bigger in Texas, then everything is smaller on Prince Edward Island. That extends right down to its country lanes, including Peters Road, which started out as a regular two-laner and then, well, petered down to just a dirt track.

Earlier, I'd stopped in to visit the office of the Canadian Automobile Association in Charlottetown and the helpful staff had offered to give me directions and a TripTik to get to Green Gables country, but I turned them down because I'm a guy and guys don't ask for directions. And after all, I have a GPS unit on my phone. Should've listened…. They say it's fun to get lost, and it can be, but I was worried for the wide tires on the rocks in the mud, not to mention the low-slung chassis.

All turned out okay, but next time I'm on Peters Road, it'll be with a dirt bike.

Day 11: Sackville, NB
Trans-Canada Distance: 1,392 kilometres

THEN: (Borden-Carleton) Many people still have fond memories of the old ferry that linked Prince Edward Island to New Brunswick, which was officially a part of the Trans-Canada Highway.

The original *Abegweit* ferry could carry almost a thousand passengers (though only 60 cars) and also broke ice during the winter on the Northumberland Strait. It was replaced in 1981 by a much larger ship that could carry 250 cars; it was also called *Abegweit*, the local Mi'kmaq word for Prince Edward Island, meaning "cradled on the waves." However, as journalist Walter Stewart observed in his book *My Cross-Country Checkup*, ferrygoers preferred to call the ship "A Big Wait," which was frequently appropriate.

The newer ship was disposed of when the 1997 completion of the 13-kilometre Confederation Bridge made a ferry service redundant. According to Wikipedia, the ship was sold to a broker in Texas, who eventually sold it to a buyer in India, and it was sailed across the Atlantic and through the Mediterranean on its last voyage, to be scrapped in India in 2004.

But the older ship found a much better fate. She was bought by the Columbia Yacht Club in Chicago, which had been refused permission by the city to construct a clubhouse on its stretch of waterfront. The club bought the ship, now called the *Abby*, and moored it permanently at its property to serve as its clubhouse. She was even given a fresh paint job a couple of years ago, so she looks good as new.

The Confederation Bridge.

NOW: (Bayfield) The ferry may still be remembered fondly, but Islanders won't trade their Confederation Bridge for anything. It's a remarkable feat of engineering that turned 15 years old on June 1.

The bridge took four years to build, and at 13 kilometres long it's officially the longest bridge in the world that crosses ice-covered water. Among other bridges over water, though, it doesn't even make the top 15 — it's dwarfed by the longest bridge of them all, the Qingdao Haiwan Bridge in China, which stretches almost 43 kilometres, followed closely in the stakes by the Lake Pontchartrain Bridge in Louisiana, at more than 38 kilometres.

The bridge is 40 to 60 metres high and 11 metres wide, with one lane each way and no overtaking allowed anywhere. Pedestrians and cyclists must travel by shuttle bus. The guardrails are just 1.1 metres tall, giving enough space to still allow drivers a view of the strait.

It was built by the private consortium Strait Crossing Development Inc. at an estimated cost of $840 million dollars — $210 million over the initial budget. The federal government still has to pay for the bridge,

Mark of Green Gables.

Mark Richardson

sending annual cheques to the consortium of $41.9 million until 2032, at which time it takes over ownership. And the consortium gets to keep the tolls till then, too.

SOMETHING DIFFERENT: (Cavendish) When tourists think of Prince Edward Island, they think of beaches and potatoes — and Anne of Green Gables. When Japanese tourists think of Prince Edward Island, they don't even bother with the beaches and potatoes.

Anne is huge here, and there are thousands of potential mementoes of Lucy Maud Montgomery's red-haired, freckle-faced creation. As Walter Stewart wrote in his book, "We have been able to avoid Anne vibrators and Green Gables garbage bags," but pretty much everything else is available, including straw hats with built-in pigtails.

Day 12: Springhill, NS
Trans-Canada Distance: n/a

THEN: (New Glasgow) I'm driving south from Sackville toward Halifax. This is so that I can double back to drive the Trans-Canada Highway from New Glasgow, NS, up to the New Brunswick border, which is the more common route for the TCH through to Cape Breton and Newfoundland, avoiding Prince Edward Island and the seasonal ferry from the island to Pictou, NS.

There are a number of places where the TCH splits in two to head in different directions. On the prairie the Trans-Canada follows the traditional route close to the U.S. border, while also breaking away west of Winnipeg onto the Yellowhead Trail that leads through Edmonton to Prince Rupert on the Pacific Coast.

In Ontario it splits into both the famous road along the north shore of Lake Superior and the older lumber road that passes through Kapuskasing and Hearst, as well as both the direct route to Kenora from

Thunder Bay and the secondary route through Rainy River. Also in Ontario, it divides west at Ottawa to follow the southern route through Peterborough or the northern route through North Bay.

And in Quebec it either goes west from Montreal to Ottawa, or north from Montreal all the way up to, and through, Val d'Or. This is not a well-known route: the spokesperson from Quebec's Ministry of Transportation didn't believe me when I told him of this alternative designation for the Trans-Canada Highway. "It's not what people think of when they think of the Trans-Canada," he said.

But I'm also coming down here so that I can drive up from Halifax on the old roads that would have existed in the early years of the last century. This Trans-Canada Trek will not only retrace the Trans-Canada Highway of 50 years ago but also the first coast-to-coast Canadian road trip, which took place 100 years ago in 1912. And while I'm at it, I'll retrace the famous coast-to-coast drive of Dr. Perry Doolittle in 1925. Doolittle founded the Canadian Automobile Association, and is also known as "the father of the Trans-Canada Highway."

Once I reach Halifax this weekend, I'll start telling the stories of those original, pioneering road trips. They were no drive in the park!

NOW: (Sackville) New Brunswick voted this summer to name its entire stretch of Trans-Canada Highway as the "Highway of Heroes," to honour Canada's fallen soldiers. It's the fifth province to do this: Ontario was the first, after which Saskatchewan, British Columbia, and Manitoba renamed portions of their TCH as Highways of Heroes.

Dedicating highways and public works to military veterans is common practice, but there was a reason for Ontario renaming 150 kilometres of Highway 401: it's the route between the air base at Trenton and the coroner's office in Toronto along which the bodies of soldiers are transported when they're first returned to Canada; people come out by the hundreds to stand on the highway's bridges to honour the passage of the hearses.

This doesn't happen at the other highways. For that reason, I think it lessens the stretch of 401 to copy the designation onto other highways, although I appreciate the honouring of our soldiers.

Ironically when Prime Minister John Diefenbaker opened the Trans-Canada Highway in 1962 he declared, "May it serve the cause of peace. May it never hear the tramping sound of marching feet."

But the name is catchy, and if it helps to remind us of what's happening to our soldiers away from Canada then that's a very good thing.

SOMETHING DIFFERENT: (Springhill) When Corporal Kate MacEachern pauses in her march along the Trans-Canada Highway on "The Long Way Home," she takes off her army boots and slides on these comfy pink slippers.

The 33-year-old single mom is marching 572 kilometres from her base at CFB Gagetown in New Brunswick to her hometown at Antigonish, Nova Scotia, to raise awareness for Soldier On, an organization that helps soldiers recover from injury.

MacEachern was seriously hurt herself five years ago in Edmonton while practising for a military event; she was a member of the ceremonial mounted division when she was thrown from her spooked horse into a post. Her head and spinal cord were damaged, she had bleeding in the brain, and was told that her life would never be the same again.

That's true: her life is very different now. "I want to show people that you can stand up to make a difference, and not just sit down and let life happen around you," she explains, sitting on the step of the RV trailer that's following her on this three-week walk. She carries a 20-kilogram pack, wears full battle fatigues, and covers at least 25 kilometres, and up to 40 kilometres, each day along the TCH, also taking time to speak to audiences about Soldier On.

"My main goal is to just get to the end of each day, and when it hurts, keep going. And when it really hurts, remember why I'm doing this."

And the slippers? She bought them a few days in when she realized she needed a break from her five pairs of boots, sandals, and flip-flops. They match a pair that she left behind at home.

"I'm not a girly-girl by any means," she understates, "but every now and again it's nice to have a touch of familiarity, a touch of pink. And they're a lot more comfortable to wear than the boots."

Mark Richardson

Corporal Kate MacEachern and her pink slippers.

To learn more about MacEachern's march, look for her on Facebook at *www.facebook.com/groups/thelongwayhome510.*

Days 13 and 14: Halifax, NS
Trans-Canada Distance: n/a

THEN: (Halifax) I'm a hundred kilometres from the Trans-Canada Highway, on the Atlantic coast here at Halifax. When the TCH was first proposed in 1949 — when the federal government sought to encourage each of the provincial governments to build the highway, since roads are a provincial responsibility — both Nova Scotia and New Brunswick insisted on the route going through their major urban centres; Nova Scotia wanted to include Halifax, and New Brunswick wanted to include Saint John. Neither city was really "on the way" though; each was a detour, and the act that passed in 1949 specified that the Trans-Canada would follow "the shortest practicable route." Ottawa did have some say in the matter, since it was agreeing to cover half the cost of construction and didn't want to pay for unnecessary additional distance.

New Brunswick finally agreed the following year on a route that bypassed Saint John. Nova Scotia held out for two more years until 1952, when, as Daniel Francis observes in his book *A Road for Canada*, in return for skipping Halifax, Ottawa agreed to construct the Canso Causeway that linked Cape Breton to the rest of the province.

NOW: (Peggy's Cove) I took a side trip today to drive past Peggy's Cove and look at the lighthouse, which is in serious need of a coat of paint. Just like the Trans-Canada Highway, neither the provincial government nor the federal government can agree on who's going to pay for this, so it stays unpainted, presenting a shabby front to the half-million tourists who visit each year.

The day is a bittersweet, though: it's Father's Day, and my two boys are at home in Cobourg, Ontario, and I should be with them. This is the first father's day since my eldest was born 15 years ago that I've been apart from them.

I've travelled a fair bit with both boys, on road trips. My eldest, Andrew, came with me to New York on my Harley when he was 11, and again when he was 12 to Washington, DC, when we rode there to meet the president. He now prefers to spend time with his friends, but in honour of Father's Day he created a Camaro using Minecraft and sent it to me on Facebook. He called me to explain how to look for it — after all, this is all from an entirely different generation.

His brother, Tristan, cut his teeth with me on the bike on a road trip to Mount Washington a couple of years ago, and this year, at 12, will be driving with me in the Camaro out west. I'll be back to Ontario in time for Canada Day, then Tristan and I will travel together for the rest of this journey. Both of us are really looking forward to this. He sent me a photo today that popped up on my phone, wishing me a happy Father's Day.

Before I left my motel room this morning — a clean room that smelled so strongly of paint that I had to leave all the windows wide open all night long — I read Ian Brown's words in the *Globe and Mail*, and they rang home across the distance that I'm separated from my own boys. "Your father stands apart, watching, the one who shows you how life works, who provides context — your instructor, your guide, your tracker, your friend … and finally your companion.".

Tristan Richardson, at home on Father's Day.

Road trips are great, but like everything in life, they come with a cost, especially on Father's Day.

SOMETHING DIFFERENT: (Seabright) Archie Chisholm says he's the only professional hammock maker in the region, and probably the country. He used to work on the line for Ford in St. Thomas, Ontario, but he and his wife Anne retired out here a few years ago to find a more satisfying life.

Now they own the Bay Hammock Company, which I drove past this afternoon on the Peggy's Cove road and swerved into to check the merchandise. And I wasn't the only one: "Father's Day for us is like Christmas Day," says Archie. "We'll sell a couple of dozen hammocks today."

He invited me to lie in one of his creations, and as soon as I settled in I knew I couldn't leave without parting with $150 to take one home. I didn't even bother to haggle — I was too comfortable. "And this one is good for the environment," Archie joked. "The rope is 'reprieve,' made out of recycled plastic bags."

Archie and Anne sold their nearby waterfront home earlier this year and have just moved into an RV that's parked alongside the hammock-construction workshop, where they spin the rope and prepare the wooden spreader bars. Once the season is over, they'll be driving that RV down south and are looking forward to the journey. They've already started keeping a blog about it, which you can read at *theaccidentalrvers.blogspot.ca*. "It'll be a big road trip, yes it will," says Archie. "You can't beat a road trip. We're really looking forward to it."

Day 15: Halifax, NS
Trans-Canada Distance: n/a

THEN: (Halifax) When Jack Haney arrived on the train here in 1912 to drive Thomas Wilby across the country on the first coast-to-coast Canadian road trip, he thought he'd be meeting up with a fellow gearhead. Haney, after all, was the chief mechanic for the REO Motor Car Company in St. Catharines, Ontario, and Wilby was the experienced journalist who'd persuaded REO to supply him with a car — and with a chauffeur, since gentlemen didn't drive themselves.

Haney turned up with three cases of clothes and supplies; Wilby had his writing equipment, a shaving kit, and a spare pair of socks. He expected Haney to purchase clothes for him as a valet might, using an REO expense account, and, after some phone calls to St. Catharines, this is what happened. Wilby also expected Haney to call him "sir." So much for being a fellow gearhead.

And then they lost the car.

The two men spent 53 days together on their road trip and they hated each other.

Wilby, standing in the car, and Haney, sitting at the wheel.

NOW: (Halifax) Today was a planning day. As I did a couple of weeks ago in St. John's, I scouted the Halifax area for a suitable boat slip so that tomorrow I can dunk the Camaro's wheels into the Atlantic (again), ready to drive across Canada to dunk them into the Pacific.

I can't use the same place that Wilby and Haney found in 1912, opposite Oland's garage in Halifax, because it's long since been filled in and made inaccessible to cars. But I did find an excellent slip at Eastern Passage across the bay, east of Dartmouth, which looks to be both shallow and forgiving.

I'll be keeping a very different schedule from those original "pathfinders," but I do plan to arrive in Victoria with my son on August 8 and dip the wheels again into the Pacific. Fifty-three days from now we'll be returning to Vancouver. Hopefully our journey will be very different from that original road trip.

SOMETHING DIFFERENT: (Halifax) I checked into my Halifax hotel, the Best Western Plus at Chocolate Lake, and was greeted at the front desk by the hotel's "Welcome Ambassador," Cocoa.

Cocoa the hotel dog.

Cocoa is a five-year-old chocolate Labrador who lives at the hotel. Her bed is behind the reception desk, and she is officially owned by the hotel company. She wanders the lobby and never seems to get excited about anything, but she has her own email address (*cocoa@chocolatelakehotel.com*) and Twitter account (*@thehoteldog*), with nearly 2,000 followers — including me, now.

Assistant Manager Tammy White was the one who arranged Cocoa's adoption as a nine-month-old rescue puppy, taken from a family that apparently didn't really want her. As a chocolate-coloured dog, she just seemed right for the Chocolate Lake hotel, Tammy says: "We were looking for something a little different and as a business decision, it all made sense. We're a pet-friendly hotel with a resort type atmosphere — Cocoa was a natural fit."

Whenever she needs a walk, there's always somebody available to take her out, and if a suitable member of staff asks, Cocoa will go away for a sleepover at the staffer's home. But most of the time, she just hangs out in the lobby, doing her job as an ambassador.

Day 16: Wentworth, NS
Trans-Canada Distance: n/a

THEN: (Waverley) The original pair of "Pathfinders," Thomas Wilby and Jack Haney, who made the first coast-to-coast Canadian road trip 100 years ago, set off from Halifax Harbour in rain and drove north on muddy roads.

It can't have been much fun in the open car, and especially not since Wilby, the British snob, sat in the back and would not have cared for conversation with Haney, the American mechanic who was provided as the car's driver and caretaker.

The roads that the two would have followed were narrow and unpaved, and no maps existed to show their route. There seemed little need — fewer than 200 cars were registered in Halifax at the time.

Instead, the duo were led north by a guide in one of those cars, and they stopped just five kilometres outside of town for a drink at an inn, where the locals' curiosity was eventually stirred when the guide told them of the long drive expected to Vancouver.

At that, everyone went outside to look at the car, while Wilby considered them with disdain. "Vancouver awoke only vague geographical associations," he wrote later. "It had no connection with their lives; it suggested a journey to the moon."

If there was to be a link between Atlantic and Pacific, most people didn't see cars as the way of providing it. In his book *The All-Red Route*, author John Nicol quotes an editorial from the Halifax newspaper that year:

> Is it reasonable, that the mass of the people, who will never own an auto, will give up the roads they made and practically own to the devil machines? Is it reasonable to believe that the legislature will take the roads of the country people away and transfer them to the rich men who may wish to make motor tracks of them...?
>
> In this province, where the country is hilly and the roads narrow, if an automobile comes suddenly over a

Wilby and Haney at Halifax Harbour, 1912.

hill in the face of a horse unacquainted with them, 10 men would not keep him from going over the bank with the wagon to which it may be attached. Automobiles have not come to stay. Just wait until they kill a few people by tumbling the wagon in which people are travelling peacefully along. They haven't come to stay on country roads, and they won't stay.

NOW: (Truro) I drove to Eastern Passage to dip the wheels of the Camaro into the Atlantic. I did this already in Newfoundland, as you can see here: *http://youtu.be/-twC2J7-M4M*, but it just seemed right to do it again, as a tip of the ball cap to Wilby and Haney. You can see today's video here: *http://youtu.be/r2gdyGp_yoA*.

From there I drove slowly along the old Waverley Road, which was the original road north from Halifax Bay, and dropped in to visit with Dave Munroe, to talk cars and motorcycles for a while. Munroe is a retired motorcycle dealer and former national chair of the Canadian Automobile Association.

It was a relaxed afternoon but perhaps too relaxed — I'd intended to follow the Waverley Road all the way through the countryside to Truro, but realized when I left Munroe's house that time was getting on; if I followed the old route I may not get to my destination near the Wentworth Valley before dark.

So, just a few kilometres north, I swung onto the main throughway and set the cruise control to 120 kilometres per hour. Every now and again, to my right, I could see the old road through the trees.

SOMETHING DIFFERENT: (Eastern Passage) I topped up my bottle with water from the Atlantic at Eastern Passage, across the bay from Halifax, Nova Scotia.

I'm topping it up because I already had Atlantic water in there from Petty Harbour, Newfoundland, which I'd gathered on the first day of this drive, two weeks ago. But I didn't have as much as I'd started out with.

After putting that quarter-bottle in the car and setting off across Newfoundland, I just left it rolling around behind the seat and forgot about it. I bought other bottles of drinking water since then. And a few days later, I was fumbling around for a bottle of water while driving and, yes, pulled up the ocean water bottle and gave it a healthy swig. Except, of course, it was a very unhealthy swig, full of salt and fish pee. I spewed my mouthful through the open window, although most of it was picked up by the slipstream and hurled back inside the car.

Anyway, today I needed to top up the bottle so that I can pour it into the Pacific. All very symbolic, though it would be more symbolic, of something, if I just spit it into the ocean at Vancouver.

The bottle of salt water is now carried safely in the trunk, and it won't be leaving the trunk until I get to the left coast.

Day 17: Moncton, NB
Trans-Canada Distance: 1,445 kilometres

THEN: (Wentworth) Bob and Carol Hyslop remember the day in 1990 very well: their neighbour Dianne Powell came over and they "were sitting on the porch, and Dianne said, 'Well, what are we going to do about the road?'"

"The road" was the planned expansion of the dangerous two-lane Trans-Canada Highway, which the government wanted to widen into four lanes alongside its existing route — right through the scenic Wentworth Valley.

The two-lane highway was built in 1957 to be part of the new Trans-Canada Highway, but traffic was much lighter then. It replaced the old through-route that was still just gravel and dirt, as well as the quickly becoming redundant rail line. But as the highway developed into a transportation route that connected Canada to both Halifax and Newfoundland, it became quickly outdated — and dangerous. Drivers would take risks passing slower traffic on the curves, and accidents were horrendous.

Mark Richardson

Bob and Carol Hyslop at home in the Wentworth Valley.

"It had to be done," remembers Carol, now a retired elementary school teacher. "Traffic was terrible. Fumes from the traffic were terrible — children were getting asthma. You couldn't cross the road. There were always accidents, but that was the only route they'd thought of to develop. They hadn't considered any alternatives. So we got a petition going. We didn't want it to go through the valley, period."

The Hyslops helped form the Wentworth Valley Environmental Protection Association, which began with about 40 members. Most of the people involved were fairly educated and well-connected people who owned property in the valley, which is well-known for its ski hill.

Once the association was formed, a letter-writing campaign was begun and didn't stop until alternative routes were tabled and then decided upon, and eventually the new Trans-Canada was built away to the west on the top of the Cobequid mountain range. It gets more snow than most places and drivers sometimes get stranded — hundreds were trapped in the snow several winters ago — but the valley itself is now quiet and clean and beautiful.

The new road was so expensive to construct that it's a toll road — the only toll road on the Trans-Canada Highway. I'll be getting into *that* touchy subject over the next couple of days in New Brunswick.

Former local-MP Bill Casey credits Carol Hyslop with making it all happen. "She had the most powerful computer in the world. It was only a Commodore 64, with a dot-matrix printer, but it got a highway moved to the top of a mountain."

Carol says she still has that computer, stored away in a box. And when she says it, Bob, a retired pilot, grins a big grin. "I'm proud of her," he says. "She took on the government and won. She proved that you really can make a difference, you know."

NOW: (Fort Lawrence) There's a small lighthouse beside the big Nova Scotia sign at the Welcome Centre on the provincial border with New Brunswick. Normally the door is locked, but Glenna Isaacs makes an exception to let me inside and explain her job.

"I count all the cars, all the trucks, all the motorcycles. I check all the licence plates and record them. There are four of us now on shifts, and we do this all year. In the summer we're busiest — we do this from 6:00 in the morning till 10:00 at night."

Glenna works for the research division of the Nova Scotia Department of Tourism, and she says there's been somebody doing this job for as long as she can remember. Since this is the only good route into the province other than on the ferry, she says it's an accurate way for the government to know who's visiting.

She's armed with a dozen clicker counters, for different kinds of vehicles and plates, and a pair of binoculars for getting a close-up of unfamiliar plates. When a car doesn't have a front plate, she swings around in her chair to watch it pass by the side window and record the rear plate.

Couldn't they just use a computer to register licence plates, like they do with the 407 toll highway north of Toronto?

"They could, but it would be very expensive," she reasons. "And computers don't see what we do, either. We can pretty much tell if a truck driver is coming in on vacation, using his rig to save on his transportation costs.

"And why spend a lot of money just to get rid of jobs?"

SOMETHING DIFFERENT: (Fort Lawrence) At the Welcome Centre, I ask about the Big Map, an enormous concrete relief map that used to be on display beside the parking lot, 50 metres long and 20 metres high. It was built in 1934 but is long since gone, removed during the Second World War, apparently, so that it couldn't show enemy spies where Halifax was.

Doug McManaman, doing what he does best.

The person who best remembers the map is Doug McManaman, who has worked at the centre for 30 years and whose dad used to tell him about it.

Doug doesn't take long to tell me that he has an unusual talent: he can balance pretty much anything on pretty much any part of his body. He took me into the supply room to demonstrate.

"I've always been able to balance things," he says. "I hold 426 world records, you know, for balancing and for shooting. Just Google my name and you'll see them."

It's true, though they're not Guinness World Records — he doesn't have much time for Guinness, which has a very time-consuming acceptance policy. Instead, he uses a New York-based company called Record Setter, and if you search his name on its website you'll see the video evidence: "Longest time to balance broom on thumb while lying on back," "Longest time to balance six toilet paper rolls on forehead whilst sitting," and so on. There are hundreds of them and other, non-balancing, records too — "Fastest time to put an egg inside a balloon and take it back out" — and a bunch of shooting records, such as "Fewest rifle shots to hit a spaghetti noodle from 50 yards away."

"If you want to do it, go for it," says Doug. "I'm 68 years old and I'm not slowing down yet. I'm going to set 500 records before the end of the year. You can do it if you try. Don't waste your life away."

Day 18: Saint John, NB
Trans-Canada Distance: n/a

THEN: (Sussex) In the earliest days of road travel through New Brunswick, the main highway led west down the Bay of Fundy from Moncton to Saint John, then turned north to pass through Fredericton and on up to Quebec.

Saint John was not bypassed until the Trans-Canada Highway was planned in the 1950s. Instead, the new TCH came halfway through from

Moncton, then turned at Sussex and stayed north to take a more direct route to Fredericton. The 1949 act that laid out the rules for the Trans-Canada said the highway should take "the shortest practicable route," and that clearly didn't include heading down to Saint John.

That route through Sussex became known as Suicide Alley, because it was often clogged with large trucks and far too many cars, all driving too fast between the two cities on two-lane roads that had not anticipated such volume of traffic. So in the 1990s the government of New Brunswick obtained federal funding to help it put through an entirely new road: a four-laner, with centre medians so wide that oncoming traffic was often hidden behind broad stretches of woodland.

There was only one problem. This was an expensive highway to construct and the government didn't have the money, so it announced there would be a toll charge to use the road.

NOW: (Salisbury) When Dr. Perry Doolittle drove down from Moncton to Saint John in 1925, in the first few days of his cross-Canada road trip with a Model-T Ford, he stopped at "a silver fox farm near Moncton." The film clip that became a record of his journey shows the foxes loose at the farm, and a couple of workers with them.

Salisbury, just off the Trans-Canada, is known as "the home of the silver fox," thanks to the prolific breeding of foxes in the area at the turn of the last century. At one time, every farmer around kept foxes, raised for their pelts, and those pelts could fetch up to $1,000 each at the auction house.

Not any more. Today there's only one farm left in the area, a small operation with about 800 foxes, and the owner is understandably nervous about talking to a journalist. Anti-fur activists are known to break into farms in the States and Europe and release all the animals. But as Ron Steeves says, those animals are only used to life in captivity and die quickly in the wild, either from starvation or out on the road.

Being a fox farmer is hard work, he says. "Nobody in their right mind would do what I've done, and I've been in the business 30 years now." There's no time off, and foxes are fickle animals, not simple to breed. "You could come home at night and just throw some food at them — and some people have no choice but to do that, to work another job — but I don't call that farming," he says.

"But I always liked the foxes. If you enjoy what you're doing, then it really isn't work."

There was another nearby farm until recently, but when owner Bruce Williams died nobody wanted to take it on. It now lies derelict.

The bottom dropped out of the industry in the late 1980s, Ron says, when fashion demands turned against real fur. Those thousand-dollar pelts sold for just $38 each in the early 90s, but the market has begun to return again with new demand from China and Russia. Now a pelt can sell for as much as $250, but there's never a guarantee of price — fur farmers don't have a marketing board to regulate prices.

Ron and his daughter, Tina, and partner, Marilyn, took me for a tour of the operation, but they didn't want me taking any photos — while they're proud of the standards they keep and the care they provide their foxes, they want to maintain a low profile. Ironic really, in "the home of the silver fox."

SOMETHING DIFFERENT: (Salisbury) I met Doug Sentell at the Salisbury Big Stop. He told me the history of fox breeding in the area, which morphed into a proud promotion of his town. And then I checked the spelling of his name.

"Two Ls at the end," he said. "Make sure you get it right — there are only five of us in Canada."

Only five? Is the name that unusual?

"Well, there's me, there's my cousin, Frank, and then my son, Peter, and his two boys. There aren't any others in this country. It's an American name, I think. There are about 37 Sentells in the States, but that's all."

Doug's been working at the Big Stop since it was opened in 1997, when his son helped design it for the Irvings. Ten years ago, he established a table staffed by volunteers that raises money for breast cancer research by selling raffle tickets toward a prize — when I visit there's a new Mini Cooper to be won.

"In nine years, that table took in a million dollars," he says. "Last year, we raised $84,000 more. Pretty good for just a table and a couple of volunteers."

Day 19: Fredericton, NB
Trans-Canada Distance: 1,610 kilometres

THEN: (Fredericton) The old Trans-Canada Highway from Moncton to Fredericton in the 1980s and '90s was a lethal stretch of two-lane road that desperately needed improvement — it just couldn't handle the constantly growing volume of traffic. There were an average of nine fatalities every year and three times as many severe injuries.

However, as New Brunswick Minister of Transport Claude Williams recalls, Brian Mulroney's federal government was not willing to put any money into the project, so the provincial government of the day was forced to go it alone. And it didn't have any money, either. That meant only one thing if the road was to be built: a drivers' toll.

Then-Liberal premier Frank McKenna was "a difficult man to deal with," says Williams. "He wanted it done and done quickly, so he said, 'It's my way or the highway!' I guess he got both."

The brand new 195-kilometre road was a marvellous piece of engineering that improved drivers' safety overnight, but the principle of paying a toll to use Canada's national highway was anathema to New Brunswickers. The toll was so despised — especially by commuters into Moncton and Fredericton, faced with a $7 charge for each car — that Bernard Lord's new Conservative government was elected in 1999 with a campaign promise to remove the tolls, which it did the following year.

But the billion-dollar price tag had to be paid by somebody, and the bill just added to New Brunswick's deficit. The 25-year contract between the province and the privately owned construction company had to be recovered, and Williams says that all New Brunswickers are still paying a "shadow toll" of about $20 million a year, based on the road's traffic.

It's an especially contentious issue because so much traffic on the Trans-Canada Highway uses New Brunswick as a corridor for Quebec and Ontario trucks to reach Nova Scotia and Newfoundland, with reduced benefit to New Brunswick. Indeed, the possibility of tolls has been raised again, but the province's politicians know it will be an unpopular proposition. According to Williams, a reasonably priced charge just wouldn't raise enough money to make enough of a dent — which means not enough to warrant the outcry it would provoke.

Political scientist Donald Savoie, of the University of Moncton, summed it up last year for the CBC: "I think New Brunswickers live in some kind of dream world where we say no to economic development, we say no to foreign involvement, and we say no to tolls," he said. "We think through black magic or voodoo economics that these things will get paid."

NOW: (Bouctouche) Claude Williams is proud of the Trans-Canada Highway in New Brunswick. He's also pleased, as minister of transport, that the province doesn't have to build any more of it. Aside from 2.8 kilometres under construction in the north, the entire 513 kilometres of the four-lane TCH through the province from Quebec to Nova Scotia is finished and complete.

There are still plenty of other roads to work on, including a $540-million construction project down to St. Stephen near the Maine border, but the Trans-Canada now just needs maintenance. That's good, because it's special.

"It may be just a name, but I think it brings an identity to Canada," he says. "It's really the only physical thing now that links all the provinces. Maybe not so much for the younger generation, but it means a lot to people like me. It's a tangible thing that really does create pride in our nation."

SOMETHING DIFFERENT: (Moncton) Just off the Trans-Canada, north of Moncton, Magnetic Hill has been drawing skeptical tourists for the last 80 years.

The story goes that locals would tell of the mysterious hill where wagons pushed along their horses; finally, in 1933 three newspapermen from Saint John drove up to Moncton to find the hill and record it for the *Telegraph Journal.*

According to the pamphlet I was given when I paid my $5 to drive on the hill,

… the intrepid trio spent most of a frustrating and often embarrassing morning stopping at the foot of every hill or minor incline they could find, slipping the car in neutral and waiting for it to roll back up hill.

By 11 a.m., vowing vengeance on the pressroom, they stopped at one last hill, just before the intersection with the old highway. Setting the car in neutral, they got out to stretch their legs a last time before the trip back to Saint John and, you guessed it … nature chose that moment to show its hand. Slowly at first, then with gathering momentum, the roadster began to roll back uphill. Moncton's incredible Magnetic Hill would now be officially recorded!

Day 20: Grand Falls, NB
Trans-Canada Distance: 1,820 kilometres

THEN: (Grand Falls) The first motorists to cross Canada, Thomas Wilby and Jack Haney, drove up along the Saint John River and then ran out of fuel near there, in the darkness, trying to make it to Grand Falls for the night.

In his later account of the 1912 road trip, Wilby wrote:

It was already dark, and there were bad hills and a swamp paved with logs ahead. To add to the charm of the situation, the petrol had chosen to exhaust itself at a moment when the car was climbing an ascent. To go upwards any farther was an impossibility; it was an equal impossibility to descend backwards, for the road behind was narrow and would lead us again into an ugly marsh that was covered with a rank growth to the edge of the wheel ruts….

Thomas Wilby, at left, and Jack Haney at right.

After some time, by dint of blowing into the tank
to gain pressure, the car was started again. Two big hills
surmounted on a thimbleful of remaining liquid power
— it was a miracle! It was a miracle too that the unfortunate chauffeur did not burst his cheeks or succumb to
asphyxia, for it fell to his lot to blow into the petrol tank
every few moments of the remaining journey....

How joyously we hailed every descent, every slight
declivity, until swamp and hills were past and the small
hotel of Grand Falls stood before us in silent welcome.

Wilby's complete account of the historic journey is a 292-page
book, *A Motor Tour Through Canada*, but it's in that second paragraph
of the excerpt that everything comes clear: Wilby, the English journalist, sat in the back of the supplied REO while his driver, Haney, did all
the work. Wilby despised Haney because he was an American and not
properly deferential; Haney loathed Wilby because he was a snob.

They were together for 53 days. It made for a long trip.

NOW: (Perth-Andover) The Trans-Canada Highway used to follow the Saint John River through the valley to New Brunswick more closely than today, but a hundred years ago the road drove right along the bank. Now the TCH passes by a kilometre or so to the west.

Kendall Nissen walks out onto the porch of his store and points toward the road on the east side of the bank. "That used to be the CP railway line," he says. "Now, do you think they'd have put a railway line along there if the river used to flood?"

No — the river has changed considerably in the last half-century, since the first dams went across it to create electric power. Since then there've been a number of floods in the town, including the deep waters of '87 and '93, which Kendall remembers from his 30 years of owning the general store. But none were as bad as the March flood of 2012. It's the reason his store is still closed.

"We've had water in the basement before, and deep water too, but it's never been above the floor. This year, it filled the basement and we had two feet of water on the main floor. It's been 12 weeks now that

Mark Richardson

Kendall Nissen in his formerly flooded basement.

we've been fixing the store and there's another month or two left before I can reopen."

There's no possible insurance for flood damage, he says, so he's been doing most of the work himself with his son-in-law, a carpenter. He's applied for compensation through the provincial government but hasn't heard anything yet; the cost for repairs is coming out of his savings.

Who's to blame? He puts the responsibility firmly on the dams.

"The river never used to flood. When they put the dams in the river, they should have done their research first but they didn't know what they were doing. It's great to have power, but it shouldn't come at this cost. I've lost all my equity now — my retirement went down the river."

The 54-year-old grandfather is optimistic for the future though, and has no plans to move. "Someday, there'll be an alternative way of creating power. I don't know what it will be, but it will be found. I have no doubt my grandchildren will see this river again, but I don't know if I will. It's beautiful on a sunset — I just want my river back."

SOMETHING DIFFERENT: (Saint John) Bricklin cars are one of New Brunswick's most memorable failures, but Mike McCluskey loves them anyway.

The gull-wing fibreglass "safety vehicle" was made for a couple of years in the mid-1970s in Saint John. The company was founded by smooth-talking auto executive Malcolm Bricklin, who brought Subaru to North America (good) and went on to import Yugos (bad). The history of the company is very well-documented: *www.bricklin.org* will tell you about the cars and *http://en.wikipedia.org/wiki/Malcolm_Bricklin* will tell you about the remarkable man.

But if you want an in-depth chat, Mike's your man. He owns three Bricklins, and will barely pause for breath recounting history and reason and trivia about the vehicles. Why are their colours uneven? Because they're not painted, they're plastic covered and the plastic fades in the sunshine at a different rate (aficionados look for these things). Why do the headlights go up and down separately? Because they're vacuum powered and there's only enough vacuum strength available for one at a time — it's known as the "Bricklin Wink."

Mark Richardson

Mike McCluskey with two of his three Bricklins.

There's more — lots more. I'd still be there now except Mike, a law-yer, had another commitment to attend. But before I left he let me drive his "safety green" car around the wide block where he lives, just to get a feel for it. And it felt … different.

"I could have got a DeLorean, I could have got a Ferrari, but then what are you going to tinker with?" he said. "There's always something breaking, but it's simple enough that I can fix it. And I can't get out of a gas station without somebody asking about it.

"It appeals to me because it's a New Brunswick car. You get a lot of recognition in New Brunswick, and a lot of satisfaction driving it in New Brunswick. Would I want to drive it to Toronto, though? Probably not."

Days 21 and 22: Quebec City, QC

Trans-Canada Distance: 2,189 kilometres

THEN: (Quebec City) Quebec's capital city isn't officially on the Trans-Canada Highway but instead lies about 10 kilometres away on the other side of the St. Lawrence River.

The earliest road-trippers came through here, of course. In 1925, Dr. Perry Doolittle, the founder of the Canadian Automobile Association and known as "the Father of the Trans-Canada Highway," practised here, putting his Model-T Ford on rails by switching over his wheels and crossing on the track of the old railway bridge. Doolittle knew that there were no roads yet built north of Lake Superior and that the only way he was going to drive across Canada that year was by using both road and rail.

Thirteen years previously, Thomas Wilby and Jack Haney crossed the river on the ferry and drove onto the steep cobbled streets of the capital, old even a hundred years ago. Wilby described it in his book:

The Camaro didn't have any problems with Old Quebec City's 2012 streets.

Quebec City is no place for a self-respecting motor car. On landing from the Levis ferryboat, there is apparently no way of mounting to the Upper Town except by a steep ascent following a winding approach to the ancient gates....

The car, heavily loaded, realized by some mechanical instinct before we did the absurdity of the unequal contest. It showed the white feather, and half-way up tried to run down again backwards. What it actually succeeded in doing was to come to a full stop athwart the line of traffic, while all Gaul collected on the sidewalks. The situation was ludicrously humiliating....

I sprang out to lighten the load. "Turn her round and back her up! Quick!" I cried, and ingloriously sought self-effacement among the onlookers. Here we were undertaking the longest road tour ever attempted in Canada, and yet we were unable to climb a paved hill...!

The car manoeuvred for the right-about-turn while I glared into a shop-window with ostentatious indifference, and decided to go in and buy something for which I had no earthly need. From the inside of the shop, I could see the car creeping laboriously backwards up the hill while the crowd panted along in its wake.

Is it any wonder that the driver, Haney, loathed his passenger?

NOW: (Rivière-du-Loup) The short stretch of highway south of here that connects traffic to New Brunswick is a billion-dollar construction project in Quebec. When it's finally completed in 2018, it will provide a four-lane highway similar in quality and safety to that in New Brunswick.

About half of the current Trans-Canada between here and the southern provincial border is still a single lane in each direction, and so has a higher-than-normal accident rate as vehicles grow impatient to pass slower traffic.

After driving through New Brunswick on excellent road, it's a lesson to drive alongside the construction and appreciate just how much blasting and levelling has to occur to build a highway. It's easy to assume, as a driver, that the route has always been fairly flat and straightforward, but when you see the dozers and backhoes among the huge rocks and rubble, smoothing out the way, you realize why road building is so expensive — and such an astonishing feat of engineering. And I'm still far from the mountains.

SOMETHING DIFFERENT: (Saint-Louis-du-Ha! Ha!) Nobody's quite sure how this small town got its name, but as best I can tell it's the only community in North America with an exclamation mark in its title.

The official story says that it's derived from an old French word for a barrier, because of nearby Lake Temiscouata, which blocked the progress of early explorers. Another story says that it came from the local native word *hexcuewaska*, which means "something unexpected" and again describes the nearby lake.

My favourite was told to me by the local tourist guide, who said that when the first explorers saw the lake, they were so taken by its beauty that they couldn't help but cry out "ha ha!"

Whichever, residents don't usually use the full name when they're talking of their town but instead just refer to it as Saint-Louis, hence the Villa Saint-Louis and the Bar Saint-Louis. That's too bad. I think that if I want a drink, I'd much rather visit a Bar Ha! Ha!

Day 23: Montreal, QC
Trans-Canada Distance: 2,445 kilometres

THEN: (Montreal) Quebec was the last province to agree to build the Trans-Canada Highway, signing on after holdout Maurice Duplessis died in 1959 and was replaced as premier by the federalist Jean Lesage.

The current stretch of Highway 20 that runs between Montreal and Quebec City is known as the Jean Lesage Autoroute, to acknowledge his contribution, though the original TCH in 1962 followed the more scenic Highway 132 along the St. Lawrence's south shore.

As part of the deal, Lesage persuaded the federal government to build the Louis Hippolyte Bridge and LaFontaine Tunnel, which is where today's Trans-Canada crosses the river. As Daniel Francis explains in *A Road for Canada*, the tunnel was a challenge for engineers:

> They couldn't dig through the thick mud of the river bottom, nor could they bore through the deep bedrock. The solution was a unique, pre-cast concrete tunnel. Sections were fabricated on land, then floated out onto the river and sunk, piece by piece, into an underwater trench. Once in position the sections were joined and the tunnel was done....
>
> The Lafontaine bridge-tunnel exemplified the spirit of innovation and expansion that were the hallmarks of Quebec's Quiet Revolution of the 1960s.

NOW: (Montreal) The Trans-Canada Highway splits here in Montreal, heading both north on Highway 15 toward Val d'Or and west along the more traditional route to Ottawa.

This four kilometres of Highway 40/15 is probably the most heavily travelled section of the entire TCH: every day, an average of 310,000 vehicles merge along the two highways. So, of course, it's under construction, which includes replacing the overpasses.

Montrealers probably wouldn't mind so much except that the current section of road that's being repaired was only fixed up fairly recently. The province's roads are in a generally poor state of repair thanks to years of neglect, highlighted in 2006 when the Concorde Overpass at Laval collapsed and killed five people. Since then, Quebec has promised almost $4 billion for roadwork.

SOMETHING DIFFERENT: (Drummondville) The sign with "the three little bums" has been beside the highway for as long as my friend Costa can remember. It's not really something you expect to see, so we dropped in this morning to visit the Centre Naturiste Domaine Soleil de l'Amitié.

Owner Roland Morin was happy to talk to us. He and his wife opened the nudist resort 25 years ago. On a warm summer's day it can be host to more than 200 people. Today was not a warm summer's day, however. It was quite cool, and threatened rain. Nobody, not even Roland, was naked.

"This is the only four-star naturist campground in Quebec," said Roland. "There are three others, but they don't have what we have," which includes a lake, two swimming pools — I saw the volleyballs — and a restaurant and bar. Bikinis and swimsuits are not allowed, just as single visitors are prohibited, only families or couples.

"Once you come in, you register, and if it's warm within an hour you've got to be naked," said Roland. "We're not all models, by any means, but you really do get to know a person when they're naked in front of you."

Roland Morin.

Day 24: Ottawa, ON
Trans-Canada Distance: 2,624 kilometres

NOW: (Ottawa) The story stays with me even today, 20 years after I first covered it as a reporter for the *Ottawa Citizen* newspaper.

Four young high school football players drove from Ottawa to visit a relative in Montreal, then left at midnight to drive home. Along the way something happened, and the driver slewed off the road into the centre median. The van careened through the grass for half a kilometre before it launched over a small river, smashed into the opposite bank, and dropped down into the water.

Three of the young men were killed instantly. The fourth, the 19-year-old driver, broke his leg and both ankles and could not climb up from the wreck, but the van was out of sight below the highway. Eventually, after more than 30 hours in the ravine, he pulled himself up to the road and was found by a passing motorist.

Mark Richardson

The Trans-Canada bridge over the Raquette River.

It's a horrific reminder of how cruel the road can be. I've always wondered what happened to that young man afterward, so today I found his mom and she put me in touch with him by phone.

John Vatsis, who now lives near Toronto, says the memory of that crash never fades: "I remember it clear as day. Greg and Blair were in the back sleeping and Gord was beside me and he was falling asleep too. I said to him not to fall asleep on me, but he did and I was tired too, so I was nodding. I kept saying, 'Five more minutes, five more minutes and I'll stop.'

"All of a sudden there was just a blank sheet of red in my head. I was looking at my friends and their eyes were closed and I knew they had passed away, their necks were broken, except Gordie, his eyes were open, but he had passed too. I didn't feel any pain. Eventually, I got the van door open, but when I stepped into the river, there was two feet of water and my ankle just twisted in it like rubber. It was crushed."

John says he crawled back into the van and slipped in and out of consciousness all day. He could hear the traffic on the Trans-Canada above and tried throwing rocks up to the road to attract attention, but the high-school star quarterback was too weak to throw them far enough. When darkness came, he crawled into the back of the van, past his dead friends, and covered himself with his brother's hockey bag for warmth. Finally, sometime in the night, "I realized that it really was now or never. I smashed the window on the other side of the van with my helmet, crawled out of the van, and used the grass and the branches to pull myself up."

He was in hospital for several months, and when he returned home he barely slept, forcing himself to work out so that he could play football again. The next year his team won the school's football trophy, but his legs hurt too badly to play more seriously; without the sport he loved, he started drinking and found drugs. He married and had children, but he says he despaired and attempted suicide. He would go back to the accident scene, where somebody had placed three crosses in the grass, and just sit and look at the river's water.

Eventually, with the help of a psychologist who he now considers one of his closest friends, John says he came to recognize the value of his children and turned his life around. A month ago he went back to the river for the first time in six years, and it was as if he'd finally moved on from the crash. He's a truck driver who tells everyone who'll listen to not drive if they're tired, and he'd like to speak to schools about the fragility and responsibility of life.

"My eldest boy is 12 — he knows about my accident," says John. "I try to teach him about these things because, you know, you think the world of your dad, but these things can happen in an instant. I hope he knows that. Just an instant and everything's changed."

THEN: (Ottawa) The old Trans-Canada Highway went through neighbourhoods and downtown areas because it was seen as a commercial boon — merchants lobbied for the road to pass by their businesses.

This wasn't too much of a problem for the first few years, in the early 1960s, but it soon became clear that heavy trucks were not welcome on Montreal's Ste-Catherine Street, or in downtown Ottawa. Even though the highway was declared open in 1962, it was obviously not yet finished — the 1962 Ontario road map shows that the TCH was still running right along Ottawa's Laurier and Bronson Avenues. It was always planned that a better highway network would offer a bypass around town for commercial traffic, but the pace picked up once the traffic began to build, and an entirely new highway was obviously needed.

In Eastern Ontario the original TCH followed Highway 17, running alongside the Ottawa River at Rockland. But Highway 417 was already under construction to speed traffic past the capital, and the highway was then extended to become a four-lane, high-speed highway all the way to the Quebec border.

SOMETHING DIFFERENT: (Ontario/Quebec border) Cross-country travellers know the curse of the Ontario border sign: You see it and think you're almost there, but in reality, you've barely begun.

It's 2,132 kilometres from the southern Quebec border to the border with Manitoba, and that's the quick way, missing out on Toronto and the entire Southern Ontario region. Truckers know the distance to be at least 24 hours of non-stop movement, while recreational drivers think of it as being a good three days of rocks and trees between Toronto or Ottawa and the start of the prairie. It'll be a lot longer for me.

Day 25: Peterborough, ON
Trans-Canada Distance: 2,869 kilometres

NOW: (Madoc) I've driven on Highway 7 between Ottawa and Peterborough many times, but never thought to stop at the sign that invites drivers to pause at the Lester B. Pearson Peace Park. Apparently, I'm not the only one.

"We only have maybe a couple a day," says Jim Burns, who looks after the place. "We might get no one for a few days, then half a dozen. But last year we had Lester B. Pearson's grandson and great-granddaughter. They stopped in, and that was nice."

The park is named after the former Canadian prime minister — and the man who ensured the completion of the Trans-Canada Highway in the mid-1960s, who I mentioned in Newfoundland when searching for his lost memorial — to honour him receiving the 1957 Nobel Peace Prize. The park is, after all, dedicated to peace.

The land was bought as an investment in the early 1950s by lawyer Roy Cadwell and his artist wife, Priscilla, but they kept it and added to it; now it's 17 acres in the woods eight kilometres east of Madoc, right on the Trans-Canada. It includes a 1.5-kilometre nature trail and a picnic area in the centre that shares space beside a symbolic burial ground for Canada's 100,000 war dead and a Japanese pagoda.

At one time, in the 1970s, the park was home to an organization called the "Institute of Applied Metaphysics." Its members claimed that UFOs visited there, but Jim, a neighbour of the park, acknowledges that he's never actually seen a UFO himself.

"Roy was involved in hospitals in London during the war and he'd seen some of its horrors, so he really wanted a legacy of peace," recalls Jim. "He died in 2002, his wife the year before. The place was becoming rundown, but we've been fixing it up — they left some funds for it to be kept open for the general public, for anyone who wants to visit."

Jim is the administrator of the charitable organization that looks after its maintenance. "We do ask for donations but we don't get much," he says ruefully. "I think last year we got six dollars."

It's a gentle place and a welcome find. Its stated intent is "to provide solace for the busy and the tired," and for 20 minutes for me on the drive across Canada it succeeded. Maybe next time I visit, I'll remember to leave a donation.

THEN: (Peterborough) Ask anybody in Ontario which highway is the Trans-Canada and chances are they'll tell you it's the 401, the wide, restricted-access road that links Windsor to Quebec via Toronto and Kingston.

It's not though. The 401 (also known as the McDonald-Cartier Freeway, after the statesmen of Ontario and Quebec) was constructed in the 1950s and '60s, but it was never to be part of the road across Canada. Like Halifax and Saint John in the Maritimes, Toronto was not on "the shortest practicable route" to link the two coasts, so its road did not qualify.

The most direct route is the old highway that runs alongside the Ottawa River, Highway 17 up to North Bay, and it's the way that the original "pathfinder" drivers took, heading toward Sault Ste. Marie.

The TCH also follows Highway 7 from Ottawa west to Peterborough, then heads north through Orillia to join the other route at Sudbury. In the '50s, Ontario's politicians knew that the vast majority of its population lived in the southern portion of the province and would be completely ignored by the Trans-Canada on Highway 17; in fact, a sizeable percentage of Canada's entire population has always lived in Southern Ontario. For them to be literally sidelined by the Trans-Canada would make the highway into a redundant oddity, hence the second route here that at least leads to the south.

SOMETHING DIFFERENT: (Ottawa) In the good old days, anybody could just drive up onto Parliament Hill, but not anymore. Security is tight. Friendly, but tight.

Mark Richardson

Tour guides having some fun on Parliament Hill.

Fortunately, a friend arranged a pass for us to drive the Camaro onto the Hill for some photographs of it beside the Eternal Flame and underneath the Peace Tower. Mounties checked on us every minute or so to make sure we weren't sticking around for long, and I'm sure those were only the cops we could see.

Finally, after I'd taken enough pictures of historic Canadiana, I jumped into the car and backed it up to drive off in front of the Centre Block's main door. "Not that way!" called the nearest Mountie. "This is one way."

I turned the wheel the opposite direction and told the cop that he'd helped me avoid a very exotic ticket. "No," he said, "I wouldn't have given you a ticket — not for a fellow Chev owner," and then told me all about the '53 Chevy he kept back home.

I was going to ask what he'd have done if I'd been driving a Mustang, but thought I'd better not push it….

Day 26: Rolphton, ON

Trans-Canada Distance: 2,834 kilometres

THEN: (Rapides-des-Joachims) Back in the first quarter of the last century, there were several adventurous drives across Canada other than the successful ones I've already mentioned in this blog. One was the road trip of Percy Gomery, who left Montreal in 1920 with his wife, Bernadette, to drive home to Vancouver. His book, *A Motor Scamper 'Cross Canada*, was published two years later and is a very funny account of their journey.

Gomery and his wife, referred to only as "the Skipper," drove to Ottawa and then north along what is now Highway 17 all the way to Sault Ste. Marie, where they then crossed into the States; there were still no roads in Canada that would take them to Winnipeg.

They stayed a night across the Ottawa River from where I am now, and Gomery's account is memorable:

Beyond Chalk River we entered wooded roads, some-

Percy Gomery and his Maxwell touring car.

times abominable and again over a pillow of pine nee-
dles, soft and silent as a billiard table. After passing a
store and a few farms we began to realize that we were
in a roadless country, practically uninhabited. As a
matter of fact our course went eighty or ninety miles
without a gasoline supply of any sort, and one hundred
and fifty miles without a garage.

Progress became retarded. About seven o'clock,
after five or ten miles in a dense, silent forest, we
emerged all in a moment on a bridge under which the
brown, turbulent waters of the Ottawa surged in the
Rapides des Joachims. The village of that name was just
around the corner....

A blind man would have known that the hotel was
bail, if his nose and ears were doing business, but we
were the sort of people who have to eat the whole egg to
know that it is old. The obvious course was to use our
excellent camping equipment, but — sigh outwardly! —
at the end of a nerve-and-liver-racking day, stitched in
unescapably by strange, unfriendly hills, and no alternative tenting ground than a foreign-speaking village,
into which a stream of loutish lumberjacks is moving
for the Saturday night spree — why! We were nervous
about it, that's all....

So we passed through a double line of degenerate
looking half-breeds, the target of their muddy eyes, to
our room. "Room!" The upper portion of the building
was merely an unfinished, dirty loft, unlighted and quite
unfurnished, except for one or two shake downs on
which a weary logger could throw his blankets.

Gomery goes on to describe a failed attempt at dinner, before
explaining

... our wooing of the god Morpheus was an amateur
effort of the rankest kind, compared to the wooing of

the god Bacchus by the lords of the forest in the bar-room just beneath those creaking boards. I must admit that the occasional concerted rendering of one of the old French-Canadian chansons lent a picturesque air, but these were outnumbered, and out-hollered, by strictly up-to-date and strictly unprintable songs of the rivermen.

I cannot say that the night hung heavily, because nothing is more enlivening than a series of fights which you hear, but cannot see, and the frequent smashing of bottles proved at least that interest was not flagging. About two o'clock Sunday morning the revelers went their noisy, uncertain way....

The rapids no longer exist — they were dammed when Canada's first nuclear reactor was built here at Rolphton in 1962, the year that the Trans-Canada Highway was opened.

NOW: (Renfrew) The road south of Renfrew is mostly twinned four-lane, as fast and as safe as you can find in Canada. And if you drive west on the TCH from Antigonish, Nova Scotia, this is the first point on the highway — after 1,540 kilometres — that you'll find a traffic light.

The road is widening and being improved. Perhaps one day it will be possible to drive across Canada without ever having to stop for anything except fuel. After all, it's been less than 70 years since motorists were even able to drive across the country, let alone on good roads. All it takes now is money....

SOMETHING DIFFERENT: (Pembroke) My Twitter followers will remember regular *@WheelsMark* tweets from Newfoundland cursing the cold temperatures on The Rock — it was only two degrees in Twillingate and rarely hit double figures. I changed my rule then, which had decreed the top will always be down on the Camaro unless it's raining, to allow me to close it when the temperature dropped into single digits.

After today, I'm thinking of adjusting that rule to allow me to close it when the temperature goes above 38 degrees, as it did this afternoon. That's 100 degrees Fahrenheit in the old measure, and plenty hot enough in an open convertible.

Day 27: Sudbury, ON
Trans-Canada Distance: 3,108 kilometres

THEN: (Deux Rivières) Percy Gomery and his wife, "the Skipper," left in late June 1920, after a sleepless night in Rapides-des-Joachims, to drive north to Mattawa.

The journey started well but quickly deteriorated as the road became more primitive. I'll let Gomery explain again from his book:

> As the world is said to grow more giddy and danger-ous with the declining sun, that execrable road did the same. For miles together it was just a succession of hidden mines into which the car plunged every few yards. Rank growth of years of grass hid both the pits and the huge rocks that threatened to tear the in'ards out of the engine if it was moving more than about two miles an hour. As it was, the car was buf-feted about brutally and so frequently was something being bent or smashed that it ceased to be a matter of comment. Then would come an awful hill, a sort of precipice cut into broad steps on which were strewn boulders about the size of perambulators. Now and then we would gain a height from which we could look a mile or two ahead over a peopleless wilder-ness of foliage, with just the suggestion of a different shade of green showing where once a road clearing had been made.

"Is that where we've got to go?" the Skipper would groan....

After dodging fallen trees, raising others and repairing bridges, I miscalculated the height of a suspended trunk and the car top was torn off. The only thing in our favour was the weather and, about five o'clock, it commenced to rain. We cast longing eyes at a rather homey boarding house at Deux Rivières station (the first hamlet in twenty-five miles), but decided to push on for Mattawa.

Immediately away from the houses, we passed into the woods again, there being no habitations or buildings whatever for fifteen miles. However, several miles along, the wheels dug their way into hopeless mire and insisted on calling it a day. I think a shovel would have saved us that night, but it was missing from our kit.

Sadly, we fished out the very necessaries, including the typewriter, and left our desolated little home with its broken running board, broken spring, broken lamps, flattened gas-tank, bent windshield and smashed top to the mercy of the rain and started back for Deux Rivières. Our arms were full of parcels; it was wet and hot; the mosquitoes were eating us alive and we were desperately tired. Several times the Skipper became hysterical. I comforted her as well as I could; in fact I recall telling her how these hardships could only make us better pals....

Believe it or not, the drive grew even worse the next day when they tackled the road again and Gomery ended up abandoning his long-suffering wife to the bears while he sought help again from a swamp. Somehow, though, they made it through and drove all the way to Vancouver. They even stayed married.

NOW: (Mattawa) Several times today I've seen billboards beside the road that ask drivers to "Remember Adam." They commemorate five-year-old Adam Ranger, who was killed on the Trans-Canada Highway in 2000, outside his home east of Mattawa.

Adam was leaving his school bus and was struck by a pickup truck that didn't stop, despite it being a clear day and all the emergency lights on the bus clearly flashing and visible for more than 1,500 metres. The pickup driver was convicted two years later of manslaughter, as well as criminal negligence causing death.

According to *www.letsrememberadam.org*, there are now more than 30 billboards sponsored by local businesses in northern and eastern Ontario, reminding drivers to stop for school buses.

———

The roundabout in Mattawa that links the Trans-Canada with Highway 533 is the first I've seen on the TCH, and it's the first to be installed any-where in northern Ontario. It was opened at the end of last November to replace a T-junction and has apparently smoothed the flow of traffic considerably. Also, apparently, truckers hate it — it's a very tight turn for a long tractor-trailer.

The roundabout cost nearly $13 million and left the small downtown area dug up for months. It's part of an 11-kilometre stretch that's being repaved and fixed up, but there are mixed feelings about all the road-work: residents want a smooth road, but there are also plans for a bypass that has merchants worried for their futures.

"We're not that worried, though," said one woman who didn't want to be named. "It's not going to happen in our lifetimes. There just isn't the money for it."

SOMETHING DIFFERENT: (Deux Rivières) It's estimated that up to 16 bil-lion logs were floated down the Ottawa River from 1830 until 1989. Yes — billion, with a *b*. Of those logs, probably 5 percent sank en route, which means, in the words of Shane Hogue, "We're never going to run out of wood."

Mark Richardson

Shane Hogue, far right, with his crew, diving for lumber.

Hogue's Deep River Lumber is one of several companies in Ontario that specialize in hauling sunken lumber out of the water. I met Hogue as he was trying to fix a leak on his pontoon boat, while his scuba divers and a truck driver waited to get back to work.

Most of the logs at this point in the river were cut after 1945, and lost when the river was flooded then to create the Rapides-des-Joachims Dam just downstream. Shane and his crew locate them with sonar, then the divers go down, search them out with flashlights in the 10-metre-deep water, and hook them to a winch on the pontoon boat.

The age of the logs can be told by the hammer stamps by the lumberjacks, says Shane. Sometimes they find really old wood from the 1800s with axe marks in distinctive notch patterns, such as Vs and turtle shapes.

Lumber salvage needs a government permit to make sure that the removal of the logs won't affect the river. Ontario charges a stumpage fee of $27 per cubic metre, but Quebec is just happy to have the logs taken from the riverbed and charges nothing, so Shane's crew works on the Quebec side of the river. It's expensive to remove the logs, though, and not everybody will pay the premium that must be charged for high-quality salvaged wood to cover its costs.

And in the wintertime, when the river is frozen — what happens then? "I have new twins," says Shane. "In the wintertime, I'm Daddy Daycare."

Day 28: North Bay, ON
Trans-Canada Distance: 2,978 kilometres

NOW: (North Bay) I returned home to Cobourg after reaching Sudbury along Highway 17. Now I'm back in northern Ontario, after driving the other Trans-Canada that leads from Ottawa to Peterborough and then up through Orillia.

Mark and Tristan set off.

Mark Richardson

I'm driving now for the rest of this journey all the way to the Pacific with my 12-year-old son, Tristan. His older brother has already been on his road trips with Dad and now is more interested in music concerts and teenage friends, but Tristan's pumped for this trip. We travel well together.

I've found part of the key to making a journey like this work well is to follow my ten guidelines. I've already done all these on the drive here from St. John's, but now with Tristan along, I'll be doing them all again.

Ten ways to turn a drive into a road trip

There are a few rules to ensure the success of any good road trip:

1. You must drive for a while on a road you've never driven on before;
2. you must stop for a coffee or for lunch at a place you've never stopped before;
3. you must travel in both darkness and light, so either leave at dawn or arrive after dusk;
4a. you must have an alternative, easier, or quicker route that you do not take; or
4b. you must have been able to take transit or fly, but chose not to; and
5. you can drive fast, but you must not hurry.

Those elements alone will turn a drive into a good road trip. They ensure a bit of adventurous exploration while also offering some sort of challenge. You don't have to go far; you can drive away now and return this evening with a sense of accomplishment. This is one welcome occasion when length doesn't matter.

But do you want a great road trip? Then you also need as many as possible of these:

6. You must cross water, preferably by ferry;
7. you must face some form of adversity, like a flat tire or heavy rain;

8. you must discover something about yourself, such as finding a relative in a graveyard or fixing a breakdown on your own;

9. you must be surprised by something; and

10. you must share at least some of the journey with somebody else.

THEN: (Scotia) In 1912, journalist Thomas Wilby and driver Jack Haney were roughly one-third of the way into their pioneering Halifax-to-Victoria drive when they came through here, and already the road trip was not going well.

"One poor devil does all the work, 'that's me'" wrote Haney in his diary. "I am hooked up with about the worst companion that possibly could be. The work is going to be hard after leaving Toronto, and not having a MAN with me, I don't know how I'll make out."

Phew! Poor Haney, the 23-year-old head mechanic supplied by the REO Motor Car Company to drive Wilby across the country in his sponsored car, was venting about the snobbish attitude of the 45-year-old English writer.

The pair were stuck for a day after their car was bogged down on a sandy hill, where a team of horses pulled them out with such heaving and jerking that the driveshaft twisted and had to be replaced by another shipped up by train. After Haney installed it — for Wilby didn't like to get his hands dirty, especially not with work intended for the lower classes — they became stuck well outside of town on "a high hill with about a 40 percent grade and a ruddy, slippery surface." Bear in mind that few public roads these days have grades of more than about 15 percent, and on the Trans-Canada, the grades are no more than 5 percent. As Haney described it: "If this was a hill, I had never seen one before; it looked more like a patent fire escape."

In winching themselves laboriously out of the sand, the driveshaft twisted again and the car eventually limped in low gear to a farmhouse near Trout Creek. "Wilby is pretty sore about the delay, is almost ready to give up," wrote Haney in his diary that night. "The trip is a farce anyway."

So what happened next? I'll tell you tomorrow....

SOMETHING DIFFERENT: (Scotia) Tristan and I drove all over this area trying to find the original site of the steep sandy hill that waylaid the pathfinder drivers in 1912. Scotia is still a small community and one of its
two railways is now a trail. We could never be quite sure we'd located the
right spot, and then we found this farm on a side road, well away from
the main highway.

"It's been Cow Shit Valley for 20, 25 years," says owner Carl Marshall.
"Everybody kept calling it that, so I figured I should put a sign up. I would
say at least 50 people every year stop and take a picture of the sign. I'll be
working away and then I'll see a car stopped and some people standing next
to the sign, and then they'll drive away. They're taking photos. That's okay."

Carl sells topsoil and his trucks have "C.S Valley Farms" written
on their doors — a nod to the good business practice of not offending
potential customers.

There were some complaints a number of years ago, he recalls, but
they didn't amount to anything. "If somebody wants to come up from the
city and complain about my sign, well, tough."

Mark Richardson

Telling it like it is.

Carl's family came to the area in 1868, walking the 70 kilometres north from the station at Gravenhurst to settle the 100 acres they were promised by the government. And that *For Sale* sign? Cow Shit Valley isn't really for sale. Carl had put the sign on a friend's bulldozer as a joke a few weeks ago, and the friend put it in turn on the farm sign. "I'll never sell," says Carl. No shit.

SOMETHING FROM TRISTAN: (North Bay) Today was my first day on the trek and my dad's 28th!

We started off our journey across this wonderful nation by driving from Cobourg all the way to North Bay. First we drove up to Peterborough so that we could enter the Trans-Canada Highway to start our trek. We passed many towns and eventually made our first and only stop on our first leg of the trip. We stopped in a little town called Scotia, which is just north of Huntsville.

We stopped because apparently back in 1912 the first people to trek across the country crashed and got stuck there, so my dad tried to find the place. On the three- or four-hour-long journey to find it, we stumbled across a place called Cow Poop Valley Farms. Me and my dad laughed, but there was a downside to that little chuckle — since my dad is a reporter, he just has to go knock on everyone's door and ask questions about this farm.

The worst part is since my dad has no sense of fashion he walks around in his white Reeboks, socks, shorts, grey hair (even though he prefers the term California blonde), and what he calls a Tilly hat. So basically he looks like the stereotypical old person.

Day 29: Blind River, ON
Trans-Canada Distance: 3,278 kilometres

NOW: (Sudbury) The Trans-Canada Highway used to run right through downtown Sudbury, but a major bypass was completed in 1995 to keep heavy traffic away to the south.

It cuts — literally — through the rocks of Daisy Lake Uplands Provincial Park, and there are cars parked on the hard shoulders where their drivers find easy access into the park. Tristan and I paused at a safe spot and climbed up onto a rock cut above the highway.

We built an inukshuk there, like many others before us. It just seemed like the right thing to do.

———

Later in the day we took a side trip to Elliot Lake to find ice cream. The Dairy Queen is behind the mall, and we paused to look at the makeshift memorial and flowers left for the victims of the shopping centre that collapsed this summer.

This is a reminder, I told Tristan, that it's important to live life to the fullest — as every day could be your last. You never know when your final day will come. If there's just one lesson I want to teach him, it would be that.

THEN: (Cutler) In 1912 Thomas Wilby and Jack Haney were meeting problem upon problem trying to drive across the province, let alone across the whole country.

They twisted the driveshaft of their REO car twice in two days, pulling it from sand on hills south of North Bay. The second time it happened they limped into the next town, where Haney, the driver and mechanic, found tools to straighten it. But when they made it to North Bay, in a time without highway maps, they learned there was not yet any road going through to Sudbury and they finally gave up. For the first time, they took the car off the road and put it on a train. The two followed separately, on different trains, taking a welcome break from each other.

That was the start of many kilometres of non-road travel for the car. After meeting up the next day in Sudbury, the two pathfinders drove south toward the lake, but found that Cutler also lacked roads. Haney wrote that they had "great sport" putting the REO on a tugboat that linked the towns of Lake Huron's North Channel above Manitoulin Island, shipping it to Blind River.

There's no trace left of the dock at Cutler, which is part of the Serpent River First Nation. I met Bill McLeod at his house near the water and he told me that local transport shipping ended in the 1950s, when the Trans-Canada linked the shoreline's communities by land. The water is difficult to navigate anyway — too many deadhead logs lying just under the surface. But he told me where the dock had been, and how to find it.

Tristan and I drove over to the old site, near a public park and the band's war memorial. We skipped rocks for a while; nothing remained to suggest that less than a hundred years ago mighty boats docked there and the place bustled with industry. Nothing whatsoever.

SOMETHING DIFFERENT: (Sturgeon Falls) Oscar Parent says he gets at least a couple of dozen carloads of people stopping every day to look at his superstretched 1968 Volkswagen Beetle. "On Sundays the parking lot is full, full, full," he adds. "It doesn't sell a lot of cars, but it sure attracts attention."

The limo is parked out front at his auto sales lot beside the Trans-Canada, which he started after moving up here six years ago to retire. But he's too busy to retire, which is why he doesn't drive the car anymore. "I don't want to use up my weekends with weddings anymore — I had too many years of that."

Oscar was a high school auto mechanics teacher in Hamilton. When he saw Paul Newman drive up to the Oscars in a stretched Beetle, he knew he had to build a car just like it. That was about 15 years ago, he thinks, pausing a long time to remember. Originally he built three, but the other two were shorter and he sold them and doesn't know their fate.

A casino from Las Vegas wanted to buy the Beetle limo, but at the time it wasn't for sale and he turned the offer down. Now, though, he'd just as soon sell it and figures it's worth $40,000 with its new souped-up engine. His son drove it last week to his prom and had lots of space for his friends — it seats 10 in the back.

"He's going to college and wants to join the OPP," says Parent. Hopefully, the future officer will never have to write a ticket against the future driver of his prom night Beetle.

Day 30: Batchawana Bay, ON
Trans-Canada Distance: 3,481 kilometres

NOW: (Batchawana Bay) The halfway point of the Trans-Canada Highway is officially here, about 50 kilometres north of Sault Ste. Marie.

I'm not so sure that this is still the halfway point, though. When Walter Stewart crossed the country on the Trans-Canada in 1965, he wrote that the road was 7,714 kilometres long. When I asked the federal Department of Transportation for the highway's official length, I was told that it's "about 8,000 kilometres," which I think they just took from Wikipedia (*http://en.wikipedia.org/wiki/Trans-Canada_Highway*). But I've been keeping a pretty careful eye on distances, and if my current reading of 3,481 kilometres is accurate, then this point is well short.

The truth is the highway is evolving, being straightened and smoothed and bypassing cities. Perhaps the Trans-Canada just isn't as long as it used to be, or perhaps my distance logs are hopelessly flawed. It's difficult to believe, after all, that the Trans-Canada is a thousand kilometres shorter than it once was. I guess I'll know better once I get to Mile Zero in Victoria.

THEN: (Sault Ste. Marie) This was the final stop for both Wilby and Haney in 1912, and Dr. Perry Doolittle in 1925, before giving up on the road across Canada for a while. There was just no road north of Sault Ste. Marie that led around Lake Superior, though construction was pressing ahead in '25 and Doolittle drove a few kilometres to the end of the road before turning back for the Soo.

In 1912, Wilby and Haney loaded their REO onto a schooner across the lake for Fort William, now part of Thunder Bay; in 1925, Doolittle swapped the wheels on his Model-T Ford for metal train wheels and took to the railway tracks, registered as a special train to coordinate with the regular locomotives.

SOMETHING DIFFERENT: (Bruce Mines) The Simpson Copper Mine Shaft only operated for one year, from 1846–47, but that didn't deter the small town of Bruce Mines from opening it to the public.

The problem is that the public doesn't know.

"You're the first tour we've given today, and we didn't have anybody yesterday," said Jenna Thompson, a university student from the town, hired as a guide for the summer. "Lots of people tell us we should have better signs. Tops, we have maybe four tours a day."

It's an interesting and well-informed tour, though the shaft is more of a four-metre-deep trench than a traditional mine. On the second week of this drive from St. John's, I stopped at a coal mine outside Springhill, Nova Scotia, and there I walked with a guide for a hundred metres or so into the wet ground. When he shut the door and turned out the lights, the blackness was absolute, darker than anything I've ever experienced. After just a few minutes in such darkness, people become disoriented, dizzy, nauseous, and fall to the floor. It was astonishing.

But the copper mine here was still a worthwhile visit, down into the coolness of the rock. It was opened for tours in 1992 but closed the last couple of years; this is the first summer it's reopened. Take a look at its website, at *www.facebook.com/SimpsonMineShaft*, if you want to know a bit more (though it's still being built), or stop in next time you drive through town — if you can see the signs to find it.

Day 31: Wawa, ON
Trans-Canada Distance: 3,638 kilometres

NOW: (Wawa) This town is famous for its giant goose, but there are actually three: the original steel and concrete statue didn't weather well after it was installed beside the highway in 1960; it was replaced three years later by the current, much lighter iron goose that is also showing its age now. And there's a smaller goose on the roof of the Wawa Motor Inn.

The goose was intended to draw attention to the community, which is bypassed by the Trans-Canada, lying two kilometres east of the highway. It was criticized as "pregnant" and foolish, but succeeded admirably.

That original nine-metre-tall goose was moved to a couple of other locations before it was bought in 2000 by Anita Young for her General Store in town. After careful restoration, two forklifts drove it carefully up the road to her property, one driving backward, the other forward, balancing the 70-tonne goose carefully between their tines. "It's a piece of our history — I couldn't just let it go," she says.

Both giant geese still pull in the tourists. They're advertised on roadside billboards for literally hundreds of kilometres — I saw one sign for Wawa outside Mattawa on the TCH, 722 kilometres east of here.

THEN: (Wawa) The 100-kilometre stretch of highway south of here to Montreal River was one of the final pieces of road to be completed on the Trans-Canada Highway, not finished until 1960. Before then, motorists had to drive the much more northern route through Kapuskasing if they wanted to stay in Canada on the road west. Most would head through the States instead.

There was a road built during the Depression from Sault Ste. Marie north, but it stopped at Montreal River. Politicians kept promising to complete it if elected, but never did. Wawa relied on the railway for its connection to the outside world, so in 1951 local merchants organized "Operation Michipicoten" to draw attention to their plight, headed by Al Turcott, who later dreamed up the Wawa Goose. Four men walked the hundred kilometres through the bush to Montreal River to prove that if they could do it, surely a road could be built. The trek took about 10 days.

One of those men was Edward Nyman, who I met today at the Seniors' Drop In Centre. He remembered the long walk very well.

"I was only 17 or so, and Mr. Turcott talked me into it. He was a great bullshitter. We had a radio and supplies were dropped in by a plane, but it really wasn't difficult. We could have done it much more quickly, but Turcott wanted the publicity so we took our time and went slowly.

"We didn't have a tent, or a tarp — just sleeping bags. It was September, so there were no bugs, but they wouldn't have bothered us anyway. We were used to the bush."

Once again, all the politicians at the group's reception dinner agreed to build a road if elected, though it took nine more years before the highway was eventually completed.

Edward Nyman.

Mark Richardson

Is the town better for the road? Edward's not so sure.

"We used to more or less trust anybody. Nobody had locks on their doors," he said. "These days, everybody has locks."

That's progress for you. He reminded me of Lloyd Adams in Newfoundland, who surveyed the highway through the bush in the 1950s. "Now we have a four-lane highway and it only takes 45 minutes to get to Walmart," Lloyd told me then. "I guess that's progress."

SOMETHING DIFFERENT: (Wawa) At Jim's barber shop, where we had our hair cut, the talk was about the black bear that was chased off the roof of the Canadian Tire store earlier this week. Bears are more of a nuisance here than ever before, and many locals blame the provincial government's cancellation of the spring bear hunt.

They also resent that neither the Ministry of Natural Resources nor the OPP will come and deal with any bear that's rooting through garbage. One guy waiting for a haircut said he had to chase away a 400-pound

Bears at the dump.

bear from his neighbour's porch that week with a slingshot and one of his young daughter's marbles.

"The dump's the worst place for bears," said Jim. "I was told there were 16 there earlier today. We've run out of space for our garbage so we just pile it on top of the old garbage and it gets higher and higher, and the bears come and help themselves."

Tristan's ears pricked up beneath the scissors and he looked at me imploringly. The 12-year-old in me felt the same way. "Where's the dump?" I asked.

It was closed and empty when we arrived a half-hour later — well, empty of humans anyway. There were at least five large black bears and a flock of birds rooting through a fresh pile of garbage about 100 metres away, on the other side of the closed, flimsy gate.

I may not have seen any moose in Newfoundland, but these bears made up for it. Now there's a tourist idea for Wawa. If people will travel all the way to Moosonee to see polar bears at the dump, surely they'll drive three kilometres off the Trans-Canada to see black bears. Except then they'll get a bit too close, and next thing you know …

Days 32 and 33: Thunder Bay, ON
Trans-Canada Distance: 4,112 kilometres

NOW: (Thunder Bay) Tristan and I stopped at the memorial to Terry Fox that's just east of town. We came here last year in an RV, and the statue was no less impressive this summer and just as inspiring.

More than $600 million has been raised to combat cancer by the Terry Fox Foundation (*www.terryfox.org*) since his death in 1980. The idea inspires many others to push their limits across Canada, including the pairs of cyclists I met in Newfoundland. But the idea is also running its fundraising course: recent articles in both *Maclean's* magazine and the *National Post* told about the glut of people cycling across the country and the hard time they have getting any attention.

Hirotaka Suzuki, walking from Vancouver to Toronto, just because.

And then there's Hirotaka Suzuki, a 27-year-old chemical engineer from Japan who's walking from Vancouver to Toronto just, well, because. "If this journey is a success, I won't get any money, but I will get to Toronto," he told me in uncertain English. After Toronto, he'd like to go to the Caribbean for the winter, or maybe South America, just to see what's there.

An OPP cruiser pulled up as I was talking with Hirotaka beside the road, about 20 kilometres east of Nipigon. The cop just wanted to check everything was okay. When I told him about Hirotaka's long walk, the officer laughed good-naturedly: "I know — he's crazy!"

The cop was probably happy he hadn't been called over to Thunder Bay, where half-a-dozen cruisers and blacked-out SUVs were setting up shop on the highway beneath the Terry Fox memorial when we passed by later.

They were almost certainly there to intercept a small group of about a dozen Hell's Angels who we met in Nipigon, all of us ordering coffee and iced lemonades and sandwiches at the local Tim Hortons.

Far be it for me to tell the cops how to go about their business, but if they'd wanted to be absolutely certain of stopping the Angels as they headed west, they could have put a roadblock at Shuniah, a short distance east along the Trans-Canada Highway. This is where Terry Fox was forced to end his Marathon of Hope, and as best I can tell from any maps, the 2.8 kilometres of TCH between Nelson Road and the road down to Sleeping Giant Provincial Park is the only point in Canada where there is no alternative road. If you want to cross the country, you have no choice but to drive on that stretch of highway.

THEN: (Neys) There was no road anywhere near the current Trans-Canada during the Second World War, although the gravel highway between Hearst and Geraldton, roughly 100 kilometres to the north, was constructed in 1943. This provided the final link between east and west; once it was complete, it was possible to drive across Canada without going into the United States.

This isolation made the area an excellent place for holding prisoners of war, and the provincial park at Neys is built on an old POW camp site. There's very little to show that up to 500 Germans were once incarcerated here, except for a few concrete foundations in the woods and a star of rocks where the flagpole used to stand.

There were escape attempts, but if they weren't caught, the prisoners would always return after a day or so, bitten by blackflies and exhausted from getting lost in the bush. One German officer even tried to skate across Lake Superior on boot blades fashioned from an old bedstead, but he soon returned like the others. Camp life was fairly relaxed, and the prisoners were well taken care of. Most escape attempts happened once the war was over and the Germans didn't want to be returned to Europe. Some even settled later in the area.

SOMETHING DIFFERENT: (White River) This town used to hold the record for the coldest temperature ever recorded in Canada: -72 Fahrenheit in 1935. That's -58 Celcius, which is way too cold to think about.

The super-frozen temperature was spotted by 14-year-old Walter Spadoni, when he saw the reading on the thermometer at Rumsey's General Store while on his way to school. School was cancelled that day.

Walter's still in White River and I found him at the Home Hardware that his dad founded as a general store in 1905. "Winter's not what it used to be — it's a lot warmer," he told me. "Our roads weren't plowed, either, but we didn't have cars so it didn't matter." White River was a bustling railway town but didn't get a road into the community until 1960, when Walter says he bought himself a Chevrolet to reach the outside world.

But town residents now question the lowest-temperature claim. "It's an urban legend," says Deb Duplassie. "It was cold enough to break the thermometer, and the mercury dropped to the bottom. We get our share of minus 30s and minus 40s, when it's cold enough to freeze your nose hairs, but who knows what the temperature really was that day?"

And even if it were true, a reliable temperature was recorded of -81 Fahrenheit (-62.8 Celcius) in the Yukon in 1947, disallowing the title. But White River doesn't need it. Now it promotes itself as the birthplace of Winnie the Pooh — the railway stop where a bear cub was bought in 1914, named Winnie after Winnipeg, and taken to the London Zoo to become an inspiration for children's author A.A. Milne and his son, Robin, which apparently is a surprise to most visitors, who assume Winnie the Pooh was created by Walt Disney.

Mark Richardson

Walter Spadoni today.

SOMETHING FROM TRISTAN: (Eagle Canyon) Today was the most fun out of all the days so far because for the first time I actually got a good night's sleep.

Also, we went zip-lining, which was just about the most fun thing I've done in my life — it wasn't scary at all. It was actually quite nice because there was a light breeze on your face and the beautiful scenery of the canyon.

Now we get to sleep in a Best Western with two separate rooms, one for just watching TV and relaxing and the other for sleeping and doing even more relaxing.

Day 34: Dryden, ON
Trans-Canada Distance: 4,461 kilometres

NOW: (Dryden) There are two Trans-Canada Highways in this region: the traditional, more direct, route 17 that passes through Dryden, and the southern route 11 that stays close to the U.S. border and passes through Fort Frances. I drove Highway 11 last year in an RV with the family and it was the most boring 400 kilometres of highway I can recall — and I've driven some remote roads. It's promoted as the "MOM" route, for Manitoba, Ontario, Minnesota, but there are no towns or lakes to break the monotony of flat trees. Too bad, because the road down to it from Kenora through Sioux Narrows, past Lake of the Woods, almost makes up for it. Almost.

This year I stayed with tradition and we took Highway 17 with all the trucks. I think it's the second-most-boring 350 kilometres I can recall. It didn't help that it was pouring rain most of the day, making the few small communities along the way look especially drab.

At least on this route there was a large sign to remind us that we're changing time zones. There was no such sign on the other road last year. Nothing. Nada. Nowt. Just trees.

THEN: (Port Arthur) In 1912 Wilby and Haney put their car onto a train to travel from Thunder Bay to Winnipeg. In 1925 Perry Doolittle put his car back onto the railway tracks to drive the same journey, for there still was no road. But in 1946, on their way to claim the Todd Medal as the first motorists to drive completely across Canada by road, Alex Macfarlane and his friend Ken MacGillivray (the former city editor of the *Globe and Mail*) were barrelling along the highway in their borrowed Chevy Stylemaster.

1946 Stylemaster Sedan Makes First Trans-Canada Trip to Win Todd Medal for Brig. R. A. Macfarlane

BRIGADIER R. A.
MACFARLANE, D.S.O.

NEARING THE END OF THE TRAIL—J. V. Johnson and George Warren of the Victoria Automobile Club, meet Brigadier Macfarlane and his Chevrolet a few miles outside Victoria and escort him into the City.

Rolling along "Canada's Main Street"—the Trans-Canada Highway—from coast to coast, Brigadier R. A. Macfarlane, D.S.O., at the wheel of a new 1946 Chevrolet Sedan, has just completed the *first* ocean-to-ocean automobile trip without leaving Canadian soil.

To win the A. E. Todd Gold Medal — offered in 1912 by the Mayor of Victoria — Brig. Macfarlane left Louisburg, Nova Scotia, with the salt of the Atlantic on his rear wheels, and after nine days of driving he arrived in Victoria, Vancouver Island, B.C., and dipped his front wheels in the Pacific, having covered

4,743 MILES

The Chevrolet used was a stock 1946 model powered with a standard six-cylinder valve-in-head engine. It was selected by Brig. Macfarlane — who held the responsible posts of Director of Mechanization and Deputy Master-General of Ordnance, at Defence Headquarters, Ottawa — because he is convinced that a "sturdy, light, economical passenger car is ideal for the average Canadian citizen." With his extensive experience of army vehicles, on the testing grounds and on active service in two wars, Brig. Macfarlane made the new Chevrolet his choice for his history-making trip — another "first" for Chevrolet!

THROUGH THE ROCKIES—The Chevrolet spent thrilling hours skirting sheer precipices and climbing high mountain roads before it encountered this quiet little valley in Canada's Rocky Range.

THE AWARD — Winning of the Todd Medal, offered in 1912, became possible with completion of the Trans-Canada Highway. It is now awarded to Brig. R. A. Macfarlane for the first authenticated journey from Louisburg, Cape Breton, to Victoria, B.C., over a specified all-Canadian route.

T46-C1

THE PACIFIC—After 4,743 miles of rapid, trouble-free driving, Brig. Macfarlane and his co-driver dip the front wheels of their Chevrolet in the Pacific Ocean—to win the A. E. Todd Gold Medal.

CANADA LIMITED · OSHAWA, ONTARIO

The successful drive in 1946.

They came in from Geraldton to the north — the last stretch of road to be completed to link the two Canadian coasts. "I would count it a good road easily travelled and free from dangers, except the possibility of dying of lonesomeness," Macfarlane wrote later.

"From Port Arthur [now Thunder Bay] to Winnipeg, the road is more interesting, but not quite as good," he reported. "That is understandable because it is much older, and in places heavily travelled. The somewhat mountainous nature of the country too necessitates a multitude of curves, and curves don't add to the pleasure or safety of driving."

The "much older" road was built during the Depression, mostly as a make-work project. And those mountains and curves no longer exist — they've been flattened and smoothed over the years. I'm sure Macfarlane wouldn't recognize it now.

SOMETHING DIFFERENT: (Thunder Bay) I got chatting with Brett Clibbery at the Starbucks in the Chapters, and he kind of set me straight on a few things.

Brett Clibbery enjoys a cup of coffee.

Tristan had just found a book he wanted to buy that listed all the possible cheats for online games, and Brett offered a sympathetic look when my son went off to pay for it. "Well, at least he's reading," I suggested. He agreed, looked at my iPhone, and waved his own iPhone. "We're not much better when you think about it," he said.

It turns out that Brett is 60, originally from Kenora, but now lives on a sailboat and travels the world. Right now he's working for a Thunder Bay company operating charter sail trips in the area, but he's looking forward to sailing south this winter. "I stay in touch with people with this," he said, waving the iPhone again. "But it doesn't replace writing a letter. When was the last time you wrote somebody a letter, with a pencil and paper?"

A long time ago. These days, my hand cramps up after a hundred words or so with a pen because I'm used to keyboards. But emails are no replacement for written words put on paper; Brett told me of an email he'd sent not long ago to an old friend he hadn't seen in years, not since they met as actors playing in *Hair* in London. "She's fairly famous now and she gets a lot of email, and she missed it when I sent it," he said. "So I sat down and wrote her a letter, just a page, telling her what I've been doing, and I sent it to her parents' address. It took a while for her to get it, but then she wrote right back. She was thrilled."

The friend was Sarah Brightman, well-known for her singing performances in the musicals of Andrew Lloyd Webber, her former husband.

I think I'll stop this account for tonight. I have a letter to write.

Day 35: Kenora, ON
Trans-Canada Distance: 4,598 kilometres

NOW: (Kenora) More trees! Maybe this really is the most boring road, after all. It might have been a challenge to build, but it's monotonous to drive now that Macfarlane's "multitude of curves" have disappeared.

THEN: (Kenora) The road linking Ontario to Manitoba was the final provincial road link to be completed in Canada, if you don't count the islands of PEI or Newfoundland. Like the rest of the prairies, Manitoba was more concerned that its roads should lead to U.S. markets in the south than to eastern Canada. A working rail line was completed in 1882, which was sufficient for moving grain to the silos at Port Arthur (now Thunder Bay), so most politicians didn't give the thought of a road much priority.

Sometime in the 1920s Ontario's minister for northern Ontario, James Lyons, bet a silk hat with the Manitoba minister of public works, W.R. Clubb, that his province would be first to complete the road to the provincial border. Considering that Ontario had to finish 50 kilometres of road through rocks and swamp while Manitoba had about 60 kilometres of fairly flat and easy highway to build, it should have been a sure thing. It wasn't.

SOMETHING DIFFERENT: (Dryden) I got an email from the PR guy at General Motors this morning. "Both of your rear tires are a bit low," he wrote. "You might want to put a bit of air in them." The GM guy was in Oshawa; the car was parked outside my hotel room in Dryden.

The Chevy Camaro that GM provided to me for this cross-Canada drive comes with OnStar, but also with an app that shows what's going on with the car right on my iPhone. Because the car belongs to GM, I had to use the PR guy's email to register the app, and he got to check out the vehicle.

"You have just over half a tank of gas," he went on, showing off now. "Your fuel range is approximately 387 kilometres. You've been averaging 11.5 litres per 100 kilometres on the car."

I can even lock and unlock the Camaro remotely with my iPhone, and, if I should ever want to, I can honk the horn and flash the lights without being inside. Pretty impressive technology that we'll probably take for granted in another decade.

Day 36: Winnipeg, MB
Trans-Canada Distance: 4,797 kilometres

NOW: (Winnipeg) Once you leave Ontario (finally!) the Trans-Canada widens and straightens and splits into four divided lanes all the way across the prairie. It's fairly easy country for road building, passing through rolling agricultural land.

There's a game you can play, driving either west or east, of looking for the last/first rock and the last/first tree. Before I discovered the prairie, I assumed that 100 metres to the east of the provincial border there would be forests and lakes, and 100 metres to the west there would be wheat. That's not the case at all, because there are more than 100 kilometres of woods and water in eastern Manitoba, including Sandilands Provincial Forest and Whiteshell Provincial Park.

The rocks end pretty quickly, though. Today I spotted the last outcrop near McMunn, which is about 40 kilometres west of the border, and that was pretty isolated.

The most easterly prairie highway trees?

The trees took another 100 kilometres or so, ending quite abruptly near Ste. Anne. Sure, there are plenty of trees around, planted in copses by hand to protect farms from the cold winter wind, but it's noticeable enough that we emerged from the forest and Tristan couldn't help but exclaim, "Look! We're on the prairie!"

THEN: (West Hawk Lake) I don't know who won the silk hat in the bet I wrote about yesterday — that's one of the reasons I'm here now, to poke through archives and discover stuff I can't find on Google or over the phone. I suspect it was the Ontario minister, for I have a news article from the day that suggests the Ontario stretch of highway to the provincial border was ready before the Manitoba stretch.

The road between Winnipeg and Kenora was finally completed in 1932, and this is its 80th anniversary. The highway was opened officially with a ribbon cutting on July 1 that year, Dominion Day, followed by a "program of sports and entertainment arranged by the two towns of Kenora and Keewatin."

Manitoba's minister of public works, W.R. Clubb, was there to represent his province and it must have been a satisfying day for him. Two years earlier, he'd written a guest editorial in the *Toronto Mail* that declared

> … a highway joining the east to the west must be a potent factor in establishing and maintaining cordial relationship…. The aviator may fly with the swiftness of a falcon from one place to another, but, cut off from all association with his fellow, he flies in the chill isolation of the clouds. Travelling by rail is a very formal affair. The traveller is hurried along by a rigid officialdom whose great aim is to detrain him at a certain destination on the moment of time specified. He has but one choice — the choice of destination.
>
> The vision of a completed Trans-Canada highway presents to the mind of the motorist many pleasing and educational prospects. He may loiter at will by many a shaded dell or meandering stream; and he may devi-

ate from this broad highway to acquaint himself with strange communities and strange peoples.

Racial animosities and interprovincial differences — and these are largely due to ignorance on the part of both in regard to the other's point of view — are being dispelled by a freer intercourse, and, undoubtedly, the construction of the Trans-Canada extension east is another great step towards perfecting our national unity.

SOMETHING DIFFERENT: (Near Winnipeg) Aha! The sign along the Trans-Canada just east of Winnipeg that declares itself to be the "Longitudinal Centre of Canada" suggests that maybe I was onto something a few days ago, when I questioned just where the halfway point of the TCH actually lies.

I thought then that we had more distance to travel, although the highway heads north and south for many kilometres in the east: along Newfoundland's west coast, up through New Brunswick to skirt Maine, and north beside Lake Superior through Wawa, where the halfway point claims to be.

However, although the TCH travels almost to Canada's easterly point, reaching St. John's, its western terminus in Victoria falls well short of the most westerly point in the country. Canada's most westerly community is Eagle Creek in the Yukon, the last stop before the Alaska border, which follows the 141st meridian, while Victoria only lies just past the 123rd meridian.

Day 37: Winnipeg, MB
Trans-Canada Distance: 4,808 kilometres

NOW: (Winnipeg) Here in Manitoba, the Trans-Canada Highway is ranked seventh on the local CAA's list of worst roads. It was voted there by CAA members, thanks to ongoing construction and poor road quality.

I have yet to drive west of here, but the road was pretty good east of Winnipeg. And Manitoba's minister of transport says he's committed to making it competitive with the U.S. interstate system, which is often the preferred route for commerce from Manitoba to Ontario.

"A number of years ago, it was the Trans-Canada in name only — it was a series of provincial highways with little federal support," says Steve Ashton. "But we've been making a significant investment in Manitoba and we've had some extra support from the feds ... we're bringing it up to the standard of interstates in the United States."

The Manitoba border crossing at Emerson, south of Winnipeg, into North Dakota is the busiest crossing west of Windsor, handling more traffic even than the crossing south of Vancouver. This is because trucking in the States is generally easier and cheaper than in Canada, especially compared to the single-lane highway of northwestern Ontario.

"You get to the border and you really notice the difference," says Winnipeg City Councillor Jeff Browaty. "They have all the money for it in the States — there are overpasses where we would have traffic lights and intersections. The speed limit is 75 miles per hour, and gas is so much cheaper."

But both politicians agree the Trans-Canada is an icon — it's still a highway that's earned its national pride. Browaty sat in the Camaro and said he'd love to take the drive across the country, to cross it off his bucket list.

Ashton's already done the drive. As a family of new immigrants from the U.K. in 1967, his mom and dad loaded their three sons into the back of a '64 Buick LeSabre the following year and drove west from Manitoba to Victoria; the next year, they drove east to Toronto.

"I'll never forget it," says Ashton, who was 12 years old for the first trip. "There were lots of motels, lots of Mountain Dew and hamburgers. I've been to many places around the world since, but those were still some of the most memorable trips I've ever taken. I would still list the trip as absolutely iconic."

THEN: (Winnipeg) I was poking through the archives of the Manitoba CAA and found a newspaper story about a Mr. H.W. White, who won a gold trophy offered by the Vancouver Automobile Club for being the first motorist to drive from Vancouver to Winnipeg under his own power. I'd never heard of H.W. White, and the clipping was not dated, but it was in a scrapbook of items from around the time of the First World War.

The article told of how White, accompanied by his unnamed wife and daughter, drove a Cadillac down to Seattle then across Washington State before crossing back into Canada from Idaho at Kingsgate. There had been a lot of flooding, and at one point the road followed a trestle bridge over Lake Pen for four kilometres where "water was lapping over the planks of the bridge for nearly the whole distance." Once in Canada, the roads deteriorated and, thanks to a couple of washed-out bridges, the party had to drive on railway tracks for three kilometres with "a solid rock wall of 50 feet high and on the other side a drop of 175 feet."

They made it to Winnipeg at an average of 25 kilometres per hour, and I thought I had a reasonable image of the drive until I read the final paragraph of the lengthy newspaper account. "In addition to the Cadillac car, the party had a Warner trailer truck, or a regular house on wheels, a complete camping outfit, containing 2 bedrooms with full sized beds, springs and mattresses, a dining room and kitchen." Presumably, this was another venture with an unnamed chauffeur, and maybe more staff, tagging along behind.

SOMETHING DIFFERENT: (Winnipeg) My friend Willy Williamson has a thing for cars, and pride of place right now in his garage goes to the Chickenmobile.

It's a 1959 Ford Thunderbird that he found rotting beside the road a few years ago. It used to be a parade car for the Chicken Delight chain of restaurants, but it spent many years in a barn after the owner tried to destroy it — the tow-truck driver commissioned to take it to the wreckers kept it instead.

Willy and some friends restored it because it seemed the right thing to do, but he isn't quite sure what to do with it now. We took it on a beer run into town and, of course, it attracted all kinds of honked horns and waves — you just can't ignore this car.

Willy and his Chickenmobile.

I suggested we swap cars, so that Tristan and I would drive the Chickenmobile for the rest of the way to the end of the Trans-Canada Highway, and Willy figured it would make it to Victoria and was happy to keep the Camaro, but there's no roof and practicality won the day. Besides, I'm not sure what General Motors would say about getting a Chickenmobile returned to them at the end of this journey.

Days 38-40: Moose Jaw, SK
Trans-Canada Distance: 5,447 kilometres

NOW: (Regina) So much for the high-quality road that Manitoba's minister of transport, Steve Ashton, told me about. Somewhere west of Brandon a flying rock scored a direct hit on the windshield, creating a starburst just to the left of my line of sight.

I was passing a truck at the time. The vehicle in front of me was waaaaay in front. There were some loose stones on the road from recent maintenance, but there wasn't much I could have done to avoid it.

We drove into Regina yesterday and I went looking for a Chip King stand, which I found in the Safeway parking lot. For $55 all in, Taylor Wandler told me he could fix the chip so that it wouldn't spread and crack the rest of the windshield. The problem is that tiny air bubbles get into the crack and can flex the glass with vibration, or with temperature change, and that can crack the whole thing.

Taylor went at it with a small drill to create a hole for the air to escape, then a suction thingee that pulled the air out. Then he injected resin into the crack to fill the glass so that it was a solid piece again. Took 20 minutes.

There's still an obvious mark on the glass if you look for it, but I'm not worried about it spreading now. And to be realistic, I've driven on lots of gravel roads so far with no issues. It's ironic this should happen on Canada's national highway.

Chatting with Taylor while he was making the repair, I realized he's in a pretty good business. His dad has owned the franchise for the last 15 years and Taylor's sister works for the company too. But think about it: there will always be windshields and there will always be stone chips in them. The price is a fair exchange for the work, and customers don't leave feeling ripped off — they blame the government, not the repair person. And most important, the business can't be outsourced. Nobody in India can fix your windshield — you've got to be right there on the spot. Pretty good business.

THEN: (Burrows) Remember Percy Gomery? I introduced him back in northern Ontario, where he was driving home to Vancouver from Montreal with his long-suffering wife, "the Skipper." When we left them, in 1920, they'd just gotten mired in a bog deep in the woods, wrecked their car, and the Skipper was becoming hysterical.

I haven't mentioned him since then because the two of them cut through the States after reaching Sault Ste. Marie. They came back into Canada south of Winnipeg — where they were stopped for speeding at 65 kilometres per hour — and quite enjoyed Manitoba, but found Saskatchewan roads to be abominable.

> Through Moosomin we loped along, over roads which, at their best, gave us something the motion of a prairie wolf, to Wapella, a typical elevator village. Starting next morning early we did a twenty-mile succession of mud-holes, which forcefully suggested to our minds a string of beads, in more senses than one. Though it might be recorded that between Wapella and Whitewood we found the one and only road-construction gang seen during the whole 500-mile drive across Saskatchewan.

Every year though, the road was slowly improving. We stayed at the farm of Phyllis and Ewen Armstrong, who had written to me and offered us a meal, and their property straddles the current Trans-Canada between Wapella and Whitewood. Prior to its construction in the 1950s,

Phyllis and Ewen Armstrong with their grandson, Jackson Mannle.

the two-lane gravel road lay parallel, just to the north of the highway, and prior to that, in Gomery's '20s, the clay road ran parallel to the south through what is now their backyard

The next morning Ewen took us four miles north to a track through a field that marks the route of the old Ellis Trail, laid out in the late 19th century as the road across the prairie. There's only a placard there now to tell anyone that it ever existed, and we found it dug up and bent by vandals. The trail is historic and protected but local farmers want it redesignated as regular agricultural land, so they can plow it in and make use of it as part of their fields. Life goes on.

SOMETHING DIFFERENT: (Moose Jaw) It's on a lot of bucket lists, and with my 50th birthday approaching rapidly, jumping out of an airplane just seemed like a good thing to do. And if I could do it beside the Trans-Canada, out on the limitless prairie, then all the better.

Tandem diving doesn't take any special training — just $250, a lot of initials on a waiver form (and a compulsory video to explain the waiver) and 10 minutes of basic information. My tandem instructor, Mark Ehrmantraut, buckled me in and his dive team partner, Pablo Moreno, volunteered to help shoot video.

Mark Richardson

High over Moose Jaw.

Mark and Pablo call themselves the Saskatchewan Provincial Free-Flight Champions, though they laugh when they do so. Mark's got nearly 5,000 jumps to his name and Pablo's trying to catch up, with 700. They love nothing better than hurling themselves from a plane toward the prairie.

"It's a huge addiction for me," said Mark, a high school science teacher who made his first jump — a tandem — in 1997. His wife jumped then, too, but she's only been a couple of times since. She's busy now as an assistant deputy minister with the Department of Highways, which seems fitting for this journey.

"Freefall is the adrenaline rush, but now we're more into the technical side of it. Every time you try something new, a new trick, you get that sense of your first jump. You can't beat it."

Pablo, a maintenance worker at the Regina Casino, agreed: "The first time I flew head down, and I was stable, it was awesome. It doesn't get any better."

And me? It's tough to describe in words, except to say the intense rush at the beginning as you plummet from 10,000 feet at 250 kilometres per hour is like nothing you can feel on the ground. Then when the instructor opens the chute at around 5,000 feet, everything suddenly becomes very calm. You're not falling — you're floating, right up until you touch the ground.

Day 41: Swift Current, SK
Trans-Canada Distance: 5,627 kilometres

THEN: (Ernfold) This rural town, 68 kilometres east of Swift Current and with a population of 21, is surely the only community in the country that lies *in* the Trans-Canada Highway.

Warren Beach has lived here almost all of his 55 years. He remembers when the road was a single two-lane stretch of asphalt, and then when it was twinned in 1973 to become a four-lane highway. But to avoid razing the town that lay to the south of the road, the eastbound two lanes branched way off to the south, as far as three kilometres away from the westbound lanes. Much of Warren's 3,600 acres of ranch land lies between the opposing lanes of highway, as does the town itself.

"It makes it kind of novel," he says. "You think of it as like the railway once was: it was the link of Canada, the lifeline of Canada. That's what the Trans-Canada is now. We've always felt here that we're kind of close to civilization, and it's because of that highway. You go 15 miles south of here and you feel you're in the middle of nowhere, but the Trans-Canada makes you feel less isolated."

Warren took me in his pickup truck along the track that formed the original graded gravel road across the province. It's the road that Perry Doolittle would have driven in 1925, when he wrote enthusiastically about the gravel and cinders that Saskatchewan spread on the sticky gumbo of its clay highways, and that Alex Macfarlane would have driven in 1946 to win the Todd Medal, before it was replaced in the early 1950s with the construction of the new Trans-Canada.

Mark Richardson

Warren Beach on the track that used to be the main provincial highway.

We spoke for a long time, while a prairie storm approached, about the decline of western rural communities and the effect of the railway and later highways on its residents. Ernfold used to be a thriving town of as many as 300 people, but it's now rundown and without facilities — just a few homes among the boarded-up houses between the Trans-Canada.

"It wasn't the highway that did that to Ernfold," says Warren. "The factors that killed this community were in place long before. It was the ongoing development of the west. Technology has changed the way we live. We don't need communities every nine miles any more. Everything is more centralized now, and it's centralized in the city — that's where the heavy capital comes from that services the rural communities. Rural life is changing. But it's all ongoing; it's still going on."

NOW: (Moose Jaw) The 60-kilometre stretch of Trans-Canada between Regina and Moose Jaw was renamed the Highway of Heroes in a ceremony last November. It's now one of five provinces to honour Canadian soldiers.

The most recent was New Brunswick, which decided to give the name to its entire 900 kilometres of TCH earlier this summer. I wrote about it earlier in this journey.

However, I still think this cheapens the original Highway of Heroes, which is the 150 kilometres of Highway 401 from the air base at Trenton, Ontario, to the coroner's office in Toronto. This is the stretch of asphalt along which the hearses containing the bodies of the fallen soldiers being delivered home travel, and people line the road's bridges to pay their respects whenever a procession passes.

No such thing happens on the TCH in Saskatchewan. Sure, the provincial government stated in a press release for the renaming that both Regina and Moose Jaw "were important bases to the Air Training Program during the Second World War and an active military presence in both cities remains today." But why not follow Nova Scotia's example and honour our soldiers by naming the TCH simply as a Veterans' Highway? This would allow the Ontario portion of road to be accorded the unique recognition it deserves.

Mark Richardson

Tristan, growing bored at 110 kilometres per hour.

SOMETHING DIFFERENT: (Moose Jaw) Tristan and I stopped at the giant moose on the edge of town to find out if it really is anatomically correct. It is, sort of, though nothing that a male moose ought to be too proud of.

While there, we met Jack and Karen from Syracuse, New York. They were holding onto a copy of today's *Regina Leader-Post*, in which there was a story about this journey. (I worked at the *Leader-Post* in the summer of 1988, so it was a little strange to be the person interviewed for the story.) They had driven out to the Pacific on American roads and were now returning along the Canadian highway.

"This is a good road — we've got no complaints," they said. I forgot to ask, though, how they fared in the Banff area, where the Trans-Canada was closed just a few days ago by a mudslide and traffic was stranded on the road overnight.

Day 42: Medicine Hat, AB
Trans-Canada Distance: 5,849 kilometres

THEN: (Gull Lake) In 1912 there were no road maps to guide the way west. Thomas Wilby wrote that he and Jack Haney were led across the prairie by a local driver along roads and tracks

> ... of the most amazing description, wheeling and returning on his course at the most unexpected places, and darting across the rough stubble while his car swayed and pitched like a tiny craft caught in a heavy swell.
>
> We bumped through sand dust and furrows, manoeuvring in wide sweeps like swift-wheeling cavalry until we picked up the railroad in the absence of any other recognized route. Gates had to be opened and shut incessantly, and it was evident that for at least half the time we were on no commonly recognized highway.

SOMETHING DIFFERENT: (Walsh, AB) At the Alberta Welcome Centre plenty of free tourist literature is readily provided, but it costs $2 for a provincial road map. Alberta is the only province to charge visitors for its road maps.

"It's just always been that way," says Victor the tourist guide. "We have a road map here from 1987, and it was two bucks back then."

NOW: (Medicine Hat) There's little doubt that Alberta's 55 kilometres of Trans-Canada, from the provincial border to here, is the best quality of highway I've driven since New Brunswick. It's smooth and wide and properly painted and well maintained — no seams of bitumen or patched-over potholes. It's four lanes, safely twinned, and a pleasure to drive underneath the big sky.

Best of all, when it's time to stop for fuel, gas is selling for $1.11.9/litre, which is a far cry from the $1.35 of Newfoundland and northern Ontario last month.

Day 43: Calgary, AB
Trans-Canada Distance: 6,142 kilometres

THEN: (Medicine Hat) Stan Sauer used to be the president of the Alberta twinning association for the Trans-Canada Highway. This is going back a few years — the retired GM auto dealer remembers that it was back in the early 1970s that the association was pressing for the two-lane TCH to be expanded to a four-lane highway, with a wide, grassed centre median.

This is significantly safer for motorists: any accidents or collisions take place among traffic that's all headed in the same direction, avoiding the deadly impact of oncoming vehicles.

He recalls that Alberta was the first province in Canada to begin twinning its highway — a relatively straightforward project since land is plentiful and, with the exception of the western mountains around Canmore and Banff, it's fairly flat and easy to build a road upon. The extra two lanes spread east and west from Calgary and were finally completed in the early '80s, making Alberta the first province to finish the four-lane TCH.

"We had the official opening but I'd hurt my back and had to phone in my comments to the ceremony," says Stan. "It was a great moment, though. The Trans-Canada had been like a goat trail in the beginning, but when it was twinned it became a proper highway. As far as we were concerned (in Alberta), it was done then. Everything since has been maintenance."

NOW: (Calgary) The Trans-Canada used to pass directly through the downtown areas of the communities along its way; the local merchants lobbied for this. In 1962, as I wrote about in Prince Edward Island, it went right through Charlottetown, coming to a halt at the lights in front of Province House. In Montreal, the Trans-Canada ran down Ste-Catherine Street in the centre of town.

This may have worked for the tourist traffic, but it was a disaster for the increasing truck and commercial traffic, which has grown ever since the scaling back of the railway system and the advent of just-in-time deliveries. Consequently, the provinces have been building bypasses to move trucks outside of town.

Medicine Hat is a good example. The Trans-Canada used to cross the river over the narrow Finlay Bridge, close to City Hall, but for a long time now it's been on a bypass to the south that keeps all through traffic out of the core.

In some communities where the road is smaller and the traffic lighter, it still passes through town. In Mattawa, for example, there's been talk of a bypass for years, but few people believe it will happen in their lifetimes because the return doesn't justify the enormous expense. Sudbury, however, is more typical of a city building a costly bypass system to ensure that trucks and through traffic stay out of downtown.

But out west both Winnipeg and Calgary are proud exceptions. They both have excellent bypasses, but they still route the TCH right through the centre of town. Truckers know which route to take. While other communities have redesignated their bypasses to be the new Trans-Canada, neither Winnipeg nor Calgary have changed the name. Good for them.

SOMETHING DIFFERENT: (Calgary) Ever since my son joined me on this journey a couple of weeks ago, he's been bashing me on the arm every time he sees a Volkswagen Beetle. "Punch buggy!" he calls out. "No punch back!"

I think he spends his whole time in the passenger seat looking for punch buggies, and he always seems to spot them first. When we found the VW Beetle limo in Sturgeon Falls, Ontario, he really went to town on my arm.

Mark Richardson

The latest generation punch buggy, in Calgary.

So when Tristan fell asleep today in the car and didn't notice the VW Beetle parked beside the road when we were in Calgary, I took a photo of it for later. "Hey, look what I saw today," I told him when he woke up. He looked at the picture on the iPhone and I saw the recognition come to his eyes, then he started to turn at me in his seat but it was already too late. "Punch buggy! No punch back!" I called gleefully. Revenge is sweet.

Days 44 and 45: Calgary, AB
Trans-Canada Distance: 6,149 kilometres

THEN and NOW: (Cochrane) In researching the Trans-Canada Highway during the past year, one name and source kept cropping up: Edward McCourt, the author of the 1965 book *The Road Across Canada*.

McCourt and his wife, Margaret, drove the highway from St. John's to Victoria the summer after it opened, when much of the road was still to be completed. The journey and its subsequent chronicle was commissioned by John Gray at the Macmillan Company of Canada, who knew McCourt as a talented writer and meticulous researcher, and the author of a series of novels set on the prairie.

Little else is known about him though, especially now. He was a professor of English literature at the University of Saskatchewan in Saskatoon, but his novels sold only a few hundred copies at their best, and after he died in 1972 he slipped into near total obscurity. This is a great shame, because his Trans-Canada book is both insightful and inspirational, and his writing is as fresh and witty today as when he and Margaret were slogging along the two-lane gravel road. I included an excerpt in Newfoundland from Rose Blanche, but now consider this, describing a detour from Calgary along the old Banff highway, Route 1A, known as the Banff Trail:

> In some respects the old highway is even more scenic than the new — at certain points it affords a broader panorama embracing the entire sweep of the Bow Valley and the mountains beyond. One of the finest views in all Canada is that from the turn-out at the top of the great hill above the village of Cochrane twenty miles west of Calgary — a magnificent expanse of river, valley, foothills, mountains, and overarching sky juxtaposed in a flawlessly balanced harmony, so flawless as to suggest a deliberately contrived artistic improvement on nature. It is a view of which no man can ever tire, for although the elements are fixed, permanent, the colour- and cloud-patterns change minute by minute so that the communicated effect is of something at once enduring and at the same time forever new.

I drove out to Cochrane today, partly to see that view but mostly to meet with Edward McCourt's son Michael, who now lives there. Michael is a retired television journalist and foreign correspondent — most recently the anchor of CityTV's breakfast show in Calgary — and he was pleased to meet with me to talk about his dad.

"There's been a glimmer of interest in the last decade," Michael told me. "Some people have asked, 'Who was this guy? And could anyone so prolific actually be any good?'"

Part of the reason for McCourt's lack of sales success was, in Michael's words, that his dad had "almost pathological shyness," unwilling to promote his books in person but preferring to let the writing stand for itself. In other respects though, McCourt was tenacious and committed: he studied for high school while working full-time on his parents' prairie farm and went on to become both a Rhodes Scholar and an exceptional athlete, accomplished in the heavy sports of discus and shot put. "His greatest expression was through his writing," explained Michael. "His last communication to me was with a note. He couldn't talk to me to tell me that he loved me, but he could write it in a note. It's how he was."

The Road Across Canada was published in the same year that McCourt found a small canker on his tongue, which was cancerous and would kill him within seven years. In that time, though, he wrote and published travel books about Saskatchewan and the Yukon, and a biography of British Army officer Sir William Butler. When he died, remembers Michael, McCourt had just returned from Ireland, working on a biography of poet W.B. Yeats.

For someone so prolific, writing was still a painstaking task: "He wrote by longhand, and sometimes he would go into his study at the house in Saskatoon with a page that was blank, and come out several hours later with a page that was still blank. But other times, he'd written a dozen pages and he would be so happy for it."

Michael has copies of all his father's books and has read them all, as has his daughter, Tracy, a fine arts major. He also has a "big box" of his father's letters and unpublished writing in his basement, some of it too personal for him to read easily, which Tracy will inherit one day. Could there be another book in there? "I don't know, but I think so," Michael says. "I hope so."

Tristan and I will be driving finally into the mountains tomorrow, so let's leave the last word with Edward McCourt, who loved the prairies with committed passion:

The plainsman like myself is likely to find his first plunge into the mountains on the Calgary-Banff run an alarming experience. Not because of the Highway gradients, which are gentle, nor the curves, which are also gentle and well-banked, but because of the sudden feeling of being separated from all familiar things. Before we are aware of what is happening the beautiful but sinister Three Sisters and assorted kinsfolk have slipped in behind us and cut off our retreat. But the valley ahead broadens — there is still room to breathe. We are not yet fenced in. Not quite.

SOMETHING DIFFERENT: (Calgary) Since we're here in Calgary, and the Olympics opened today in London, it seemed only right to visit the Olympic Park from the 1988 winter games.

There's a special deal where you can both ride a zipline down the route of the ski jump and take a bobsled ride down the mountain course for $99. After throwing myself from an airplane over Moose Jaw and riding a zipline through Eagle Canyon in northern Ontario, Tristan and I could hardly resist.

The zipline was very fast — in fact, too fast. Unlike Eagle Canyon, when I ground to a halt five metres from the end and had to be dragged onto the dock, I slammed into the end much harder than anyone expected. It's advertised as a 140-kilometres-per-hour ride, but I'm sure I was going faster than that.

I was glad to be able to film the zipline run with my GoPro, where the helmets were fitted with camera attachments. At Eagle Canyon cameras were forbidden and they told me at length that it's because the government won't allow them — they're too distracting. This is nonsense, of course, as we both knew, but it was their canyon and their zipline and they could make whatever rules they wanted.

Days 46 and 47: Glacier National Park, BC

Trans-Canada Distance: 6,452 kilometres

THEN: (Frank, BC) The original pathfinders in 1912 could not follow a road anywhere near the current Trans-Canada — it just didn't exist. Instead, Thomas Wilby and Jack Haney stayed south of Calgary and headed west from Lethbridge, Alberta, but they needed a guide to point them in the right direction. As driver Haney wrote later in *Motoring* magazine:

> The road winds in and out, up and down. Our pilot suggested a hinge in the centre of the car to facilitate making some of the turns. Near Frank, we narrowly escaped going into a torn out bridge. We had lost the road and were playing blind man's buff around some large stones. We finally came to the conclusion that we were getting no nearer Vancouver so we stopped to collect our few remaining wits and look around. Our guide climbed out of the car and went prowling off into the dark, but soon returned with the information that a light could be seen around the hill behind us. We soon had our directions again and found that we were only a quarter of a mile from a small town and three miles from Frank.

Ten years later, Percy Gomery and his wife, the Skipper, followed a similar route along a narrow, mountainside road, recounted in his book:

> Spurting up a hill both steep and high, we found ourselves tossed on to a narrow ledge of a precipitous, shrub-grown hillside. Here, clearly, passing another vehicle was impossible. A quarter-mile of such road sounds a short drive, but it is a long time to hold one's breath! We drove fully that distance with chances of turning out quite hopeless. Then appeared a man on horseback, seemingly a cowboy, though I have never been sure. Passing room for even an equestrian was out of the question....

Laying the end of the reins smartly on his horse's flank, the rider forced his animal about twenty feet up the steep incline, turned to face us and scornfully switched his arm westward ordering me to proceed. Although I did this very cautiously, the manoeuvre was too much for the prairie steed. Just as we came underneath, he became frantic and, first plunging, then rolling, he came down on our little car, smashing the mudguard, one headlight and a few more ornaments of out mantelpiece. The rider was thrown heavily, his legs being well under the front axle when the car stopped. The horse had scrambled up and made off down the trail ahead of us, bleeding freely from a long cut in the hind quarters. The cowboy, his very muteness declaring his rage and humiliation, leaped to his feet and ran after the beast....

NOW: (Banff) An estimated 74 million tonnes of rock slid onto the town of Frank in 1903, obliterating the community and killing 80 of its 81 residents. During July 2012, just before we passed through, a torrent of mud the size of a football field slipped down from the mountainside and buried the Trans-Canada Highway just west of Banff. Hundreds of people were inconvenienced when the road was closed for cleanup; nobody was hurt.

Mudslides and avalanches do kill people here, but they're better controlled then ever before, just as communities are better designed than they've ever been. But even so, the ones that do the damage are rarely anticipated.

We drove through Kicking Horse Pass today, the highest point of the entire Trans-Canada Highway at 1,627 metres (5,338 feet). Its two lanes are relatively narrow and it has tighter 40-kilometre-per-hour curves than the Trans-Canada near the Cabot Trail that I questioned in Nova Scotia. There are chainmail sheets hung high beside the road to catch falling rocks. The road is downright dangerous for bad drivers in poor weather, but on a blue sky day like today, it felt safe, secure — and marvellous.

Mark Richardson

At the entrance to Kicking Horse Pass.

SOMETHING DIFFERENT: (Canmore) I ran a contest on my *@WheelsMark* Twitter account, asking followers to send me their Trans-Canada road trip stories. The winner was Jeremy Kroeker in Canmore. I met with him over dinner last night to give him some restaurant gift cards as a prize.

Here's his winning story:

> My old Chevy S-10 would not start. After two days of bone-shattering cold in Canmore, Alberta, the battery was dead and you couldn't dent the oil with a chisel. CAA sent someone out that night, but it was hopeless.
>
> I needed the truck in the morning, though. I had promised to meet my parents in Medicine Hat, Alberta.
>
> The truck lacked a block heater, so I set up my camp stove under the oil pan to blast it with fire. My friend Tom connected a battery booster. Soon the engine turned over, but it still wouldn't catch.

Tom had a solution, though — ether. He opened the air filter and sprayed into my injectors. The can hissed while I cycled the ignition.

I had just leaned out of the window to remind Tom about the stove when the night lit up with a "WHOOOOF!" I imagined Tom with a freshly blackened face, still bent over the engine. But he was ok so I kept cranking.

Except now my engine was on fire. I jumped out to help Tom throw snow on everything. After that we stood there, just staring.

"I think we almost had it," said Tom.

I got back in the cab and Tom kept spraying ether until the engine started.

The truck made the trip the next day and I met my parents, but on the way back there was a horrible knocking. I called a few mechanics who all agreed that the cost of repairs would be greater than the value of the truck.

So I tried driving home, but the truck finally died along the Trans-Canada Highway. I called CAA again. Then I sold my S-10 to a tow-truck driver from Brooks, Alberta, for $2 — which is less than I paid for the can of ether.

SOMETHING FROM TRISTAN: (Canmore) Yesterday was great because we went whitewater rafting for about two hours. It was so fun because there was great scenery, lots of drops, and even lots of little nooks and crannies for us to do cool stuff like flip the boat.

I think that by far the best part was that I got to use the water gun that was at the bottom of the raft to squirt other people. At the end of the ride we also played a game called trust, where basically you use the T-grips at the end of your paddle to hook onto someone else's, then lean back as far as you can and see if the person tries to let go. My dad tried to let go but I stayed in the boat so he just pushed me in with his paddle.

We also tried to climb up on an iron bridge so that we could jump off, but my dad pulled me down into the water. After the ride was over we were all treated to pop and cookies, which was great if you ask me.

We have also been going through the beautiful Rockies, which is fantastic because tonight we are in a hotel room that looks right out over the Rockies. And tomorrow is my dad's birthday and I have a special gift for him, so I'm excited to see his face tomorrow.

Day 48: Rogers Pass, BC
Trans-Canada Distance: 6,479 kilometres

THEN: (Rogers Pass) Happy birthday today to the Trans-Canada Highway! It was opened 50 years ago on July 30th, when BC Premier W.A.C. Bennett declared BC Highway 1 open at the Rogers Pass. At that moment, in front of 7,000 people, he snipped a ribbon near Revelstoke, 70 kilometres west of here, and the current road was open to be driven across the country.

There's no celebration of this here today, though. That's because Bennett's provincial ceremony had pipped the federal government to the line — the official opening of the Trans-Canada Highway took place September 3 in front of another 4,000 people, at the summit of the pass in Glacier National Park. That's when Prime Minister John Diefenbaker tamped down a patch of asphalt and declared the Trans-Canada Highway to be open. Except that motorists had been driving it for the previous five weeks.

This was all due to money squabbles. Bennett wanted the feds to pay a greater portion of the cost of construction, but Diefenbaker refused, reasoning that Ottawa was already covering the complete cost of construction through all national parks, including both Revelstoke and Glacier on the run through here to Golden.

"There was one of the most peculiar, self-centred actions that I've ever known," Diefenbaker said later of Bennett's ceremony.

The national ceremony was not without its own controversy, though. It was snubbed by both Newfoundland and New Brunswick, both of which claimed, not incorrectly, that their portions of the road were far from finished. In Newfoundland, 600 kilometres of the 1,000-kilometre highway had yet to be paved and Joey Smallwood was holding out for more money. He got it, too, and went on to "finish the drive in '65."

———

The Rogers Pass took six years to construct through some of the most challenging terrain in the country. There was already a CP Rail track through the pass, completed just before the last spike was pounded home in 1885, but it was a dangerous track — hundreds of people were killed by snowfalls and avalanches before it was pushed underground by the eight-kilometre Connaught Tunnel in 1916. I'll write more about the TCH's remarkable construction tomorrow.

NOW: (Rogers Pass) The Rogers Pass is not the highest point of the highway — that's the Kicking Horse Pass east of here. It's still plenty high though, at 1,330 metres (4,364 feet) and gets an average of more than eight metres of snow every season.

Much of the challenge of the road's completion was to protect it from avalanches. This is done with — among other things — explosive charges to knock out large accumulations of snow before they have a chance to build, and cone-shaped barriers of concrete scattered on the mountainside to dissipate sliding snow.

Most obvious though, are the snow tunnels: literally, above-ground tunnels that mean any avalanches pass over them and into the valley below, without affecting the road itself. When I drove through here last summer, I assumed these were actual tunnels that cut through the cliff face, but they're not. They weren't created to ease the road's construction but to prevent its destruction.

SOMETHING DIFFERENT: (Rogers Pass) And happy birthday to me, too! I was born at the exact moment that Bennett was cutting that ribbon 50 years ago. People tell me I was born to drive this highway, but I think I'm just up for a good road trip.

I spent a lot of time on the phone today, talking in 16 consecutive interviews with local radio hosts, each for 10 minutes or so. Phew!

The interviews were booked through the CBC's syndication service, and then they called to make sure I was still available. The problem was, the only fitting place for me to do this was from here on the summit of the Rogers Pass, and I really needed a landline. My cell phone had five bars of connection on it because there's a Bell tower up here, but then a thunderstorm rolled in and the service dropped off, usually just as I was getting introspective. CBC Charlottetown in PEI lost me during a live broadcast and never did call back — sorry.

There's a hotel up here though — who knew? — and I booked a room that came with its own phone for the final dozen interviews. It's an older hotel, built just 18 months after the opening of the pass. A couple

Mark Richardson

The view through the window of the hotel.

of fellow travellers driving home to Vancouver from Halifax met me up here after keeping in touch throughout this journey and they took Tristan off for lunch while I set things up. Thanks, Ed and Bev.

SOMETHING FROM TRISTAN: (Rogers Pass) Today was my dad's birthday and I bought him a gift that I think he enjoyed. It is basically a guy riding a motorcycle that you can put a wine bottle in to create the body.

We are staying in a hotel right on the Rogers Pass and he's definitely happy about that because of the whole "birthday at the same time as the opening of the Rogers Pass" thing.

Also, at our hotel, one of those tourist buses showed up and a whole bunch of people unloaded and were fascinated with the gophers. They took lots of pictures of me because I happened to be feeding the gophers at the time they showed up, so maybe I'll be famous in China.

Day 49: Revelstoke, BC
Trans-Canada Distance: 6,550 kilometres

THEN: (Revelstoke) For decades, the Rogers Pass was considered impractical for a highway, thanks to its mountainous terrain and heavy snowfall.

In the 1930s, when the government committed to building a road across the Rockies, it preferred the Big Bend route that followed the Columbia River north from Revelstoke in a 300-kilometre loop back down to Golden. The road was built at great cost and mostly by pick and shovel, taking 11 years to construct through the Depression. It opened in 1940, not quite complete. But it was never very good — narrow, dusty, corrugated gravel, and little scenery to speak of, except dense stands of cedar and the occasional glimpse of the river. Most drivers avoided it, instead putting their cars on the train that ran through the pass.

Journalist Bob Metcalfe once described a drive in 1960 in which he

> ... joined a motoring fraternity whose Big Bend stories
> improved with age.
>
> They're stories of broken springs, shock absorbers,
> axles and nerves; cracked windshields, lights, sumps
> and composure; lost tailpipes, mufflers, hub-caps and
> reason. Skeletons of cars, stripped of worthwhile parts
> and abandoned after major mishaps, lie forlornly at
> intervals by the roadside; others that went over steep
> embankments lie where they came to rest, battered
> wrecks....

And so, instead of continuing to maintain an untenable highway, the decision was made in 1956 to build the new Trans-Canada through the Rogers Pass. The initial budget was estimated at $22 million for the 143 kilometres of road, though after seven years — two years longer than expected — the total cost came in at about four times that, or a million bucks a mile.

As Daniel Francis describes in his excellent book *A Road for Canada*, "The challenges of the Rogers Pass section were many. The site was isolated. Weather was unpredictable. Terrain was steep, criss-crossed by deep gorges and prone to landslides. Workers got used to blasting a stretch of right-of-way only to have it buried under a new pile of rubble cascading down from the slopes above."

Sound familiar?

The road through the Rogers Pass was officially opened 50 years ago yesterday by BC Premier W.A.C Bennett. He and the Alberta minister for roads cut a ribbon across the highway about 13 kilometres east of Revelstoke, and declared the road open. According to the *Revelstoke Review* that week, "An actual count of those around the ceremony placed the number at close to 3,000. In addition, it was estimated that 30,000 people were in the seven miles of cars lined up two abreast on each side of the ribbon, waiting to get through."

Most important, though, the newspaper account went on to add: "Tourists who lined the highway in the miles of procession breathed a sigh of relief when the minister of highways announced at the official opening that the highway would remain open." For as I wrote yesterday, the Trans-Canada itself was scheduled to open five weeks later by Prime Minister Diefenbaker at a ceremony on the summit. Officially, Bennett held the provincial ceremony early because he would not be unable to attend the national event; unofficially, BC and Ottawa were arguing about money. Like anything ever changes.

At that federal ceremony on September 3, the local MP welcomed the distinguished visitors and made the pointed observation that 347,000 people had already entered the park in the 33 days since the road was opened. I'll bet that went down well.

NOW: (Revelstoke) Mayor David Raven says the traffic safety issues of the two-lane Trans-Canada in his town are starting to become personal. On average, seven people are killed every year on this section of the highway up to the summit of the pass, and it's due to excess speed, driver fatigue, and the design of the road.

"Living on the highway, we service it but we also have to pick up the carnage," he says. Last fall, when Raven realized that four people had been killed on the road so far that year, he says he braced for the news of the next three to die and sure enough, a mother and her two children were killed when their car was flattened by a semi-trailer. The road becomes narrow and slippery when there's snow built up on its sides, and the drivers just run out of room to avoid accidents.

"I made a presentation to the premier just this morning about it," he told me over coffee. "I asked her for a commitment to the highway. It's not for us or the city, but for the skiers who come to visit." There are 2,000 to 3,000 skiers driving the road every day in the winter, sometimes up to 10,000 in a day. On average, 12,000 vehicles drive the road every day throughout the year, with more than half of them being commercial traffic. Those are far more than the highway was designed to carry.

Ideally, the road will be twinned to four lanes all the way through, as it is on the prairie and through Quebec, New Brunswick, and Nova

Scotia, but the cost is excessive in this mountainous region: roughly a billion dollars, and that's just the section from Revelstoke to the summit.

So what did Premier Christy Clark say to the mayor's request? "She said, 'Thanks Dave,'" he sighed. "It'll be costly to build it, but it has to be rebuilt and maintained anyway. The money should be spent now to get it right."

SOMETHING DIFFERENT: (Revelstoke) I saw a sign on a store window here in town that said: "Check the 'Stoke List' for days open. You don't use the 'Stoke List' — ask a young person."

"Stoke list"? This made no sense to me. Nor would it to Tristan, but I asked him anyway, since he's 12 years old: "Hey — what do you think the 'Stoke list' is?"

"Dad — we're in Revelstoke. It'll be online. It'll be a list of businesses in Revelstoke," he said.

I can't bring myself to check if there's a commercial website for Revelstoke but I'm sure there is. And did I mention that I just turned 50?

Day 50: Kamloops, BC
Trans-Canada Distance: 6,762 kilometres

NOW: (Sicamous) Most of the Trans-Canada between Revelstoke and Sicamous is two lanes. Get stuck behind a truck — or more likely at this time of year, an RV — and you'll be following it for a while. Traffic moves at the speed of the lowest common denominator. This encourages risky overtaking, but it also squeezes oncoming vehicles together.

Rob Young knows this, which is why he refuses to take his bicycle on that stretch of road. He's on a cycling trip with his 14-year-old daughter, Claire; they left their home in Nelson on Saturday and plan to return Friday. They've been cycling the mountain roads under their own power, but when I met them today they were looking for a sympathetic pick-up-truck driver.

Mark Richardson

Rob and Claire Young.

"When you're driving it, it's just too narrow," he said. "The shoulder's dodgy and it's too narrow for two vehicles to pass with bicycles on the side of the road. I don't like to even drive it in a car, but I won't take a bicycle on it."

THEN: (Creston) Far south of the future Trans-Canada, and making much slower progress, Thomas Wilby and Jack Haney finally ran out of road again in 1912 at the railway town of Yahk. It was nighttime and as they had first discovered at North Bay, there were places where there just weren't any paths or trails to follow.

But they didn't give up — there was still an alternative, thanks to a pair of guides and the railway.

> We were astride the glittering rails which were to lead
> us along the intense darkness of the Yahk Loop.
>   There was a gasp as one felt the first forward plunge
> of the car and the white path of acetylene light shot

before us into the immense shadows of that forest wilderness. Four pairs of eyes strove to pierce the distance ahead and behind; and every nerve was strained in listening for a possible monster of steel and steam which might dash down upon us at any moment from around a curve, or catch us in its swift career from behind! Muscles were tense, ready for the leap to a precarious safety at the first sight of an approaching headlight....

They didn't realize in the dark that they were on the edge of a cliff with a 160-metre drop, descending at times so steeply that the car would roll under its own weight. They endured "incessant and infernal jiggling and jolting that shook the teeth and vibrated through the spine." Sometimes they got stuck between the ties and would have to jack up the car to roll forward again; their rear tires were ripped apart by the ties' spikes. After they finally found a road again, it took another three hours to drive the 19 kilometres through the soft gravel of the narrow road through the Goat River Gorge, listening to the loosened stones bouncing down to the river 150 metres below.

They arrived in Creston at 3:00 a.m., exhausted, though Haney was still able to summarize the drive in his understated diary: "Had h__l of a time getting to Creston.... Fourteen miles on ties, and up some fierce hills."

SOMETHING DIFFERENT: (Craigellachie) For much of its route the Trans-Canada follows the rail line across the country, and here, 46 kilometres west of Revelstoke, is where the Last Spike was hammered home in 1885 to complete the original link across the country.

The caretaker of the site, Lorne, located for us the actual spike on the track that was "the last spike," right beside the monument, but pointed out that the original spike was removed immediately and replaced with another, slightly larger. He also pointed out that in the famous photo of the spike being hammered in by CPR director Sir Donald Smith, there seem to be a number of empty places on adjacent ties that are still waiting for spikes of their own, so perhaps it was not truly the final piece of the railway.

And just for good measure, he mentioned that the track has been replaced seven times since 1885. It reminded me of the street sweeper who's proud that he still uses the same broom after years of service, though the brush has been replaced 10 times and it's on its ninth handle.

"There are a lot of stories here that never made it into the history books," Lorne said, and told us about 26 Chinese workers who died of starvation in their construction camp later that winter of 1885. Apparently the train driver was under orders not to stop for any reason between stations, and the out-of-work labourers were snowed in and couldn't leave the camp. "You won't find that story written anywhere," he said. Well, true or not, I'm proving him wrong now....

SOMETHING FROM TRISTAN: (Revelstoke) Today my dad left his keys on the counter for like the billionth time. It was on the counter of the McDonalds in Revelstoke.

At first we couldn't find them so my dad was a bit concerned, as he should be because we don't want anyone driving off with our only mode of transportation. Someone had turned them in, but that was a close one. I can only imagine how bad it would be if we lost them.

Day 51, Abbotsford, BC
Trans-Canada Distance: 7,114 kilometres

NOW: (Hope) The fast way through from Kamloops to Hope is on Highway 5, the Coquihalla Highway. It's four-to-six lanes all the way through, shaving 60 kilometres off the distance with a 110-kilometre-per-hour speed limit, and was completed in the mid-1980s, when it was opened as a toll road. The tolls were ended in 2008.

This means that the Trans-Canada Highway in this region, which continues west for about 70 kilometres to Cache Creek and then follows the Thompson and Fraser rivers south to Hope, is really more of a tourist route now than a commercial road. It's the only part of the entire route across the country that's been sidelined like this, but this is not a bad thing — the road twists through the canyons and offers fabulous scenery to drivers. It's not the quick route, but it is the stunning one.

Just don't be in a hurry. While there are plenty of three-lane over-taking sections, there are also plenty of sections where the two lanes are in the opposite direction, climbing a long hill, and double yellow lines prevent overtaking the slow-moving lumber trucks and RVs that must descend more slowly for their greater weight and more challenged brakes.

THEN: (Lytton) The roads through the Fraser River canyons were not designed for cars when Thomas Wilby and Jack Haney drove them in 1912. They'd been built a half-century earlier for wagon trains to bring supplies to the gold miners at Barkerville, and they were as basic and precipitous as they could be.

The two pathfinders, with a third man named Earl Wise, made slow progress to Lytton from Lillooet, continuing so late into the night that their acetylene tank ran dry, which meant they had no headlights. Their kerosene-powered parking lights were too dim to be of use, being up high beside the windshield, but they could not just park and wait for dawn because their car filled the entire road, blocking the way for the horse-drawn freighters that needed no lights.

Consequently, described Wilby in *A Motor Tour Through Canada*, Wise took one of the kerosene lights and

> ... stretched himself at full length along the mud-guard next to the outer edge of the road, reached out his arm so as to bring the lamp close to the ground, and boldly gave the signal "Go ahead!" Ten miles on one's stomach, holding a light over a sheer drop of hundreds of feet is a devilishly unpleasant role! Inch by inch we crept on. Moment by moment the poor fellow grew stiffer. A sudden jolt and it seemed as if we must throw him down the bank. A flicker of the light,

and it seemed as if we all, car and passengers, were already over the brink. We were incessantly rounding a series of bluffs, twisting and turning in short, sharp curves that shut out the road ahead. Conversation languished. The unfortunate man progressing on his stomach gave vent to his emotions only in occasional grunts.

Eventually they arrived safely in Lytton, where they had no choice but to put the car on a train south to Yale. The Canadian Pacific Railway was built through the Fraser Canyon on the site of the old Cariboo Road and it was not driveable. It would take the pathfinders only three more days to reach Vancouver. Their night drive would be the final true challenge of their long journey.

SOMETHING DIFFERENT: (Hell's Gate) British Columbians know the story of Simon Fraser exploring the region here in 1808, passing through the narrow and deep Hell's Gate section of the canyon on wooden planks suspended by ropes from high above.

The road that finally made its way through the canyon was the Cariboo Road, which also literally hung off the cliff face in many of its steeper sections. It was used only by horse-drawn wagons, but it was important to keep the horses calm on the trail high above the river. When the railway replaced it, tunnels were blasted through the rock to avoid hanging the rails out in mid-air.

These days it's a simple drive to Hell's Gate but visitors still get to suspend themselves over the canyon. Gondolas drop 175 metres down from the road to the opposite side of the river, and a suspension bridge crosses back over the fast and deep water. The river here has three times the volume of Niagara Falls, apparently, and its crossing can still bring butterflies to the stomach.

Day 52: Vancouver, BC

Trans-Canada Distance: 7,179 kilometres

NOW: (Vancouver) The Pacific at last!

I've been dreaming of this day ever since leaving the Atlantic slipway at Petty Harbour, Newfoundland. The CBC came out to film me then, and the CBC came out again today to film our arrival, when we dipped the wheels in the ocean 52 days later near Kitsilano (you can watch the video at *http://youtu.be/l1FUbbybExY*). The weather was warm and sunny, and everything went so smoothly I was worried that disaster was imminent, especially as we drove through endless construction and the heavy traffic of a long weekend — but so far, so good.

Of course, we're not quite there yet. The Trans-Canada Highway continues west from here over the ferry to Vancouver Island, and down to Victoria. We'll be leaving for the island on Monday.

Mark Richardson

Dipping into the Pacific.

THEN: (Vancouver) Thomas Wilby and Jack Haney drove into Vancouver on October 14, 1912. Their arrival was keenly anticipated and dense crowds welcomed them to City Hall.

The reporter from the *Vancouver Sun* wrote glowingly that the REO was

> ... stained with the evidence of strenuous travel, covered with mud and oil and grease, but with every component part performing its allotted function regularly and efficiently as the day it left the Nova Scotia coast, the Halifax to Vancouver Reo automobile, bearing the banner of the Canadian Highway Association with Mr. Thomas Wilby at the wheel, drove up in front of the Vancouver hotel at six minutes to four o'clock yesterday afternoon. The total distance travelled was 3,900 [miles].
>
> No tour by motor car has caused more widespread interest. The difficulties attendant upon the expedition

Thomas Wilby and Jack Haney in Vancouver.

were almost incalculable. Mountainous, unmarked country had to be traversed, water courses crossed where there were no bridges, country travelled where there were no trails or paths, and in many cases railroad rights of way and grades taken in lieu of roads. It meant the survival of the fittest. A slight defect in mechanical construction, a moment's relax of vigilance in driving over dangerous trails, and the object of the tour would have been at naught.

Wilby and his mechanician Mr. F.E. Hanley [*sic*], were both deeply tanned by exposure to all sorts of weather, but beyond that there was little to indicate either in the crew or the car the magnitude of the undertaking or the unusual nature of the trip.

SOMETHING DIFFERENT: (Vancouver) We were met in Burnaby by Lorne and Irene Findlay and their son Peter, who gave us an escort to the ocean in their 1912 REO and 1962 Plymouth Valiant.

Mark Richardson

Peter and Lorne Findlay.

The REO is the exact same model of vehicle that Wilby and Haney drove across the country a hundred years ago, and in 1997 the Findlays drove their car in a re-enactment of the journey from Halifax to Victoria. They were accompanied by John Nicol, now a journalist with the CBC based in Toronto, who wrote about the trip in his book *The All-Red Route.*

The Findlays' REO attracted all kinds of attention on the streets of Vancouver as we followed it in to Vanier Park, where we dipped the wheels into the water of False Creek, under the Burrard Bridge. The REO had to be hand-cranked to start but then it ran smoothly all the way — though the smell of the exhaust reminded us that it wouldn't pass any emissions test these days.

Following the old car was quite something, and to recognize the challenge that faced Wilby and Haney, especially on the rough mud and sand roads and steep hills that set them back time and again.

When the pathfinders drove across Canada in 1912, the car ran fairly well with few incidents of reliability; when the Findlays drove the same route in 1997, they didn't even get a flat tire.

Days 53–55: Port Alberni, BC
Trans-Canada Distance: 7,204 kilometres

NOW: (Nanaimo) The ferry from Vancouver's Horseshoe Bay to Nanaimo on Vancouver Island is officially part of the Trans-Canada Highway, linking the mainland road with the island road down to Victoria.

The arrangement is the same in the Maritimes, where the Newfoundland ferry at Port aux Basques and the PEI ferry at Wood Islands are both considered an integral part of the highway.

Everyone told me to book the ferry ride long in advance, because this is a holiday weekend, so I did and paid a deposit of $15. When I rolled up today there wasn't much traffic, and the cashier asked me straight away for $80.70 for the ticket — a car and two people.

"I've already made a reservation and paid a $15 deposit," I told him, expecting him to knock down the figure by 15 bucks.

"Okay," he said, "but it's still $80.70. That $15 is just a reservation fee — it's not a deposit."

So I spent $15 to make everyone's lives easier — mine and the ferry organizers. But why? What's the justification? What costs $15 here? Nothing, that's what. I think it's a complete rip-off to be charged $15 to hold a ticket, which goes back to standby anyway if you don't turn up within 30 minutes of sailing. Even Ticketmaster's online concert reservations are cheaper — $10 for the privilege of printing your own ticket — and I think that's also a rip-off.

People have been asking me about the justification on the Trans-Canada Highway for tolls, as with the Cobequid Pass section in Nova Scotia and the Confederation Bridge and ferries, and I've been answering that these are costly services that have to be somehow paid for. However, an additional $15 for buying your ticket in advance is unconscionable. If anybody at BC Ferries can justify the cost in any way whatsoever, please let me know.

Incidentally, the line up for the ferry at Nanaimo back to the mainland was hugely long — anyone without a reservation was out of luck. So why the additional charge to drivers for helping everything run smoothly?

THEN: (Port Alberni) This was the original westernmost point of the Trans-Canada Highway, back in 1912 when a group of motorists drove here from Victoria, Nanaimo, and Vancouver. The Malahat Highway from Victoria had just been opened and this was as far west as anyone could drive in Canada.

Speeches were made by various politicians and auto enthusiasts, and a highway was called for that would link the country by road instead of just rail. There were only 50,000 licensed cars in Canada at the time, but the number was growing rapidly and the motorists could see the future.

On that day, May 4, a signpost was constructed and planted at the end of the road in Alberni; it read simply CANADIAN HIGHWAY and an arrow pointed east, back down the road. Some of those in attendance, including Albert Todd, the creator of the Todd Medal that I'm carrying, predicted that the Trans-Canada would be complete within five years or so.

But there was to be controversy within just a couple of days. Residents of the rival neighbouring town of Port Alberni stole the sign and replanted it within their own city limits a couple of kilometres away. Not to be outdone, the Alberni residents promptly stole it back again.

And as Thomas Wilby described in *A Motor Tour Through Canada*, when he and Jack Haney arrived in Alberni in the final days of their journey: "The treasured post was tenderly restored to its rightful place on the inlet, and a bull terrier, fierce and aggressive of disposition and sharing the local indignation, was chained to it to keep watch and ward over the outward symbol of a road that is yet to 'weave province with province, to interlace people with people.'"

Today the long-amalgamated town of Port Alberni is more than an hour's drive northwest from the Trans-Canada, which runs between Nanaimo and the terminus in Victoria. But it has a special place in the highway's history nonetheless.

SOMETHING DIFFERENT: (New Westminster) After meeting Lorne and Peter Findlay on Friday, I was invited to join them for the annual meet of the antique chapter of the Vintage Car Club of Canada. Peter said, "There's room in my 1911 Cadillac," so how could I refuse?

I set off first with Paul Carter in his 1908 Cadillac, because he was on his own and I was to be his navigator, reading out the turn-by-turn directions for the 30-kilometre route. "My brakes aren't very good, but I go slowly and the parking brake's okay," he said, none too reassuringly. There were no seatbelts — at least half a century would pass before anybody even thought of them — and not even any electrics. If this Cadillac was The Standard of the World that it claimed to be, the standard wasn't very high back then.

Paul gave a hard turn of the hand crank, the engine fired without too much protest, and we putted off up the road. But something didn't sound right. Every shift between the three gears clanged and banged and ground away, and Paul didn't look very happy. Then after about eight kilometres, while coming down a hill and distracted by the horrible noises coming from beneath our feet, the brakes failed and we bumped into a Ford Model T truck that was stopped at a junction. Impact speed was perhaps one kilometre per hour, but even so Paul uttered a few timeless epithets and I hitched a ride with Steve Eremenko in his '57 GMC truck while the Cadillac gave up on the day and headed for the garage at home.

Steve and I covered another eight kilometres before we pulled up behind Lorne Findlay, who was looking under the hood of the 1932 REO sedan he'd brought along for the day. It had just coasted to a halt and Lorne, a retired mechanic, diagnosed a vapour lock in the gas line caused by excess heat. It was a very hot morning and he'd forgotten to open the ventilating louvres on the hood. "I should have brought the '12 REO," he lamented. "It's gravity fed — the fuel line would have been fine." It took 15 minutes of draining gas and blowing into the line to push the fuel through before the engine finally caught and we carried on to the finish.

Mark Richardson

The '11 Cadillac.

After ice-cream floats everyone headed home, and I hitched a lift with Peter Findlay back to his house, where the Camaro was parked. Five of us set out in his '11 Cadillac; only two arrived. After — you guessed it — about eight kilometres, the car just ran out of power on a steep hill and ground to a halt beside the road.

Peter jumped out and cranked for all he was worth in the hot sun, sweating and straining as we all watched from the cool shade, but the engine wouldn't catch; we were parked uphill and it was too dangerous to turn it around for a push start. With great regret, Peter suggested that the three of us who had other engagements would do better to just walk over the hill for the final kilometre back to his home.

"This isn't the way I wanted it to end, but sometimes it just can't be helped," he said as we shook hands to say goodbye. As I walked away, an elderly woman walked up to him on the sidewalk and grasped his arm. "I used to drive in a car just like this!" she cooed. "I wish I still had it."

"Want to buy this one?" I heard him say. "It's going cheap today."

Later that day, he sent me an email. "Yes, I made home on my own power," he wrote. "Cliff and I sat there for what seemed like ages (basically entertaining the passersby with their cameras). Eventually I remembered that I had a gallon of gas in the back, so I dumped that in and managed to get it running again. I guess it was low on fuel for hauling five people up the hill, but it should have been ok. The heat didn't help. Anyhow, I got it home and stuck it in the garage and I'll try it in the morning when I have more energy and both of us are a little cooler.

"After today, I hope you have a better understanding/appreciation of what the early travellers were up against. I still marvel at the thought that we were able to do 5,000 miles in Dad's REO with virtually no problems."

After today, so do I. So do I.

Day 56: Duncan, BC
Trans-Canada Distance: 7,250 kilometres

NOW: (Duncan) The town of Tofino would have liked me to drive on west from Port Alberni to reach the end of the Trans-Canada. It claims to be the Pacific terminus of the highway, but this is just a claim — it's not, despite the sign down by the wharf that declares it as such.

The drive to Tofino is an extra 125 kilometres west, but it's slow going. Highway 4 is a narrow two-lane highway that twists and turns in places between rocky outcrops, and it doesn't allow for higher speed. Even so, the town lobbied back in the 1930s and '40s to be the end of the Trans-Canada, and there are those who say that the municipality was double-crossed by politicians in Victoria. The sign went up back then and it's not about to be taken down.

But there's nothing official about the town's declaration. Just because it's the farthest west point on southern Vancouver Island and opens onto the Pacific Ocean that's not enough to qualify it as the TCH's endpoint. In fact, the Trans-Canada already reaches farther west than Tofino: The Yellowhead Highway, Route 16, which splits away from Route 1 in Manitoba west of Winnipeg and passes through Edmonton, is officially considered part of the Trans-Canada Highway. It ends at Prince Rupert, north of Vancouver Island and much farther west.

THEN: (Port Alberni) I poked around the town's museum this morning and discovered there may have been more to the story of the 1912 gathering than I knew about yesterday.

The neighbouring towns of Alberni and Port Alberni were fierce rivals. When the Canadian Pacific Railway company decided in 1907 to build its station in the newer community of Port Alberni, the Alberni residents figured that to make up for losing the railway they would pitch for the new highway.

So which came first: the town of Alberni approaching the motoring organizations, or the motorists suggesting the highway to the town?

Modern historical accounts favour the latter, but it seems more likely it was the former.

Either way, it's no big deal, except that it may be that the first germ of the idea for a Trans-Canada Highway came about from the petty jealousy of two small chambers of commerce, far away from any corridors of power.

SOMETHING DIFFERENT: (Coombs) Tourists know the "Goats on the Roof" Country Market as just that — a very popular place to stop that just happens to have goats grazing on its roof. It's a restaurant and a well-stocked store full of gourmet foods and bizarre souvenirs, and several other stores for surf equipment and jewellery and all things popular with West Coast visitors.

But how did the goats get there in the first place?

"It's a building that's built in the Norwegian style with grass on the roof — our heritage here lends itself to that — and it's not uncommon there, in Norway, for goats to graze on the roof," says manager Arthur Urie.

"In 1971 or '72, the fall fair literally ran out of space for its goats, and so the owner of the store offered to put some of the goats up on the roof during the fair and it just stuck. All of a sudden, people starting driving by to see them, and then they stopped at the store, and so there have been goats up there ever since."

There are currently three goats that live on the roof, taken up there at the end of April and brought down again to more level pasture in mid-September. Daniel and Hendrik are the four-year-old twins, while Willy is the larger goat, older by a year. They're social and popular — as many as 5,000 people visit the store and peer up at them on a busy summer day.

And at the end of the summer, what happens to the goats?

"They'll go out to pasture," says Arthur. "Don't even suggest anything else! These goats are my wife's pets — don't even breathe anything different or she'll be down here with a big stick to protect them!"

Day 57: Victoria, BC

Trans-Canada Distance: 7,370 kilometres
Trans-Canada adjusted distance (including ferries): 7,605 kilometres

NOW: (Victoria) Tristan and I drove the final hour right through to the very end of the highway this morning — or is that the very beginning?

The sign says "Mile 0" and as journalist Walter Stewart wrote in 1965, "The Trans-Canada Highway [is] the world's only national roadway that has two beginnings and no end. You start from Mile 0 on Water Street in downtown St. John's, Newfoundland, drive 7,714 kilometres, and finish up in Beacon Hill in downtown Victoria, where the sign reads — guess what? — Mile 0. Neither city wanted to be at the tail of the procession, so we made a road with two heads and no foot. Very Canadian, very sensible."

That was close to 50 years ago and much has changed since. The road no longer starts in Newfoundland in downtown St. John's — as I

Mark Richardson

Also at Mile 0.

discovered on the first day of this journey, it starts at the dump — and the distance is now more than a hundred kilometres less, including the salt-water distance covered by the ferries that connect Newfoundland and Vancouver Island to the mainland.

While the eastern end of the highway is purely practical, because Newfoundlanders generally consider it to be the road across their province rather than the road across Canada, the BC terminus is still graceful and beautiful, once it's finished pressing through Victoria's congested downtown. The Trans-Canada ends at Beacon Hill Park and today there was a young deer grazing under the trees near the sign. It seemed a world away from the moose I was warned about constantly back east.

Driving the Trans-Canada is no longer a challenge; anyone with a driver's licence and a vehicle can do it. Rush along and it can be covered in a week, though those are long days filled with driving and not much fun. But slow it down and everything changes — the highway becomes a necklace across the country, linking the Canadian provinces and their people to each other in a tangible, physical, highly visible way. There's still a romance to be found on the road if you want to look for it: it's right there beneath your feet, under your tires, waiting to show you Canada.

THEN: (Victoria) The Malahat Highway, which goes over the mountain just north of Victoria, was completed in 1912.

Thomas Wilby and Jack Haney drove it to arrive at the provincial capital on October 18 that year, 53 days after leaving Halifax, and I'm sure the end could not come too soon for the pair. They'd grown to despise each other.

They went straight to the provincial capital building beside the harbour to deliver various pieces of mail to the mayor that dignitaries had given them along the way, and then to the coast to pour their remaining bottle of Atlantic water into the Pacific. That night, as in Vancouver, they were feted as heroes — or at least Wilby was. Dinner was at the Pacific Club, and Albert Todd — of the Todd Medal — spoke, then the deputy minister of public works, and then Wilby.

In his book, Wilby says,

The end of the trip (for Wilby and Haney in Victoria).

It was after the car had been stripped of the appurtenances of travel — after the speeches of the banquet at the Pacific Club — that I strolled out under the stars to the Douglas obelisk in the Parliament Grounds ... Sir James Douglas, who had pre-visioned the day when vehicles would make the crossing of the Canadas to the Pacific! Linking east with west — a trail from Hope to the Kootenay across the Rockies, meeting at Edmonton a similar road built westward from the Atlantic — a great highway should cross the continent by which emigrants from the maritime provinces might have easy access to British Columbia. As in the days of Sir James Douglas, so now Canada needs the Transcontinental Highway for the unification of her peoples.

It was not that simple, though. Wilby and Haney left separately to return east on separate trains and never spoke to each other again. Indeed,

Haney rarely spoke of the adventure at all. And it would take another 50 years before the Trans-Canada Highway would be declared open, and another decade after that before it could really be considered finished.

And it's still not finished, though it is complete. It will never be truly finished, because it's improved, widened, straightened, smoothed over with every year that passes. In another hundred years, who knows what the Trans-Canada will look like, or what route it will take? But it will be there, linking the provinces, lending its iconic route to the country, never to be taken away.

SOMETHING DIFFERENT: (Victoria) Louise Rouseau lives at Mile 0 House, right opposite the famous sign in Beacon Hill Park. Her cousin owns the building and she visited in 1961 on her honeymoon, the year before the TCH was opened officially. Is there anything different about living right at the end of the Trans-Canada Highway?

"Oh yes," she says, "there most definitely is. You see a lot of stuff here — some sad, some good. One guy drove off the end of the road, down the cliff. He was trying to kill himself. It didn't work though and he walked back up on the steps.

"People come to see the Terry Fox statue. Many tour buses stop here, but I don't know if they know that it's the end of the Trans-Canada. I tell them if they ask. Sometimes, when I'm out with my granddaughter, we get swarmed by a tour bus. We get our photo taken — a lot."

Epilogue: A Trans-Canada Highway We Must Take for Granted
Cobourg, Ontario
Trans-Canada Distance: 7,605 kilometres

NOW: (Cobourg) Last month, halfway through this Trans-Canada journey, a journalist asked if I'd had the "aha!" moment yet. That gave pause for thought, but I had to accept it had not yet hit.

Mark Richardson

The Douglas Obelisk, in front of the British Columbia Legislature.

In fact, it took right up to the last moment of the drive before it struck in Victoria, at the end of the highway.

In 1912, when Thomas Wilby completed his All-Red Route in the REO and had just been feted in Victoria, he wrote that he "strolled out under the stars to the Douglas obelisk in the Parliament Grounds ... Sir James Douglas, who had pre-visioned the day when vehicles would make the crossing of the Canadas to the Pacific!"

So after writing that late-night account from the comfort of a hotel room beside that same provincial legislature, I decided to copy Wilby and stroll next door to look at the obelisk under the stars. Downstairs in the lobby, I asked the night manager where on the grounds the Douglas obelisk would be. He looked at me blankly. He Googled it with no success. He shrugged. "Maybe if you ask security there, somebody will know," he suggested. "Perhaps it's inside and you'll need to wait till morning."

I walked next door anyway. It was after midnight and the city was quiet, but the Legislative Building was lit up like a Christmas display.

And right in the front, just a step from the sidewalk at the very centre of the grounds beside a grand Sequoia, was a seven-metre-tall obelisk in memory of the former BC governor Sir James Douglas.

Back at the hotel I mentioned this to the night manager. "Of course," he said. "I can see it now. I see it every day. I just take it for granted, I guess."

And like Douglas's vision, that's the Trans-Canada Highway in this new millennium: long dreamed of, roughly achieved, and now taken for granted. Of course there's a highway across the country — why wouldn't there be?

Most of the people with whom I've talked about the Trans-Canada over the past few months are surprised to realize it's only 50 years old. Very few can appreciate the challenges of driving across the country before the highway was built. Nobody can imagine a country without it, though they may not use it themselves for more than a local trip. But that's the beauty of the TCH: In a nation as varied and regionalized as Canada, it has a different relevance for everyone while still providing a connection that's more than just a strip of asphalt.

In Newfoundland it's the road across the province. In Grand Falls a woman told me, "I use it all the time just to get anywhere. But my sister, she lives in Canada and she only drives it when she comes to visit me here." By "in Canada," she meant on the mainland, in Ontario, where roads thread everywhere. Then she thought for a while, and added, "I guess I'd use it to go visit her, too."

In New Brunswick it's a fast and wide four-laner that hustles cars and trucks safely between the Maritimes and the rest of the country. The highway is very well-built because it was always going to be a toll road, paid for by the truckers and tourists. Then politics got in the way and New Brunswickers have been paying for it ever since.

In Quebec it's the road to the Gaspé, again fast and wide through the flatland south of the St. Lawrence but an afterthought for the short stretch southeast of Rivière-du-Loup into New Brunswick. That's chang-ing now at great expense, as the traffic fatalities of a two- and three-lane road can no longer be ignored and an all-new highway is being con-structed alongside the old. It's also the road to the north, for the TCH splits at Montreal to lead to both Ottawa and up to Val d'Or. "No it doesn't," argued the man at the transport ministry, incorrectly, when I asked about this. "Ask anyone in Quebec and they'll tell you the Trans-Canada is the road to Ottawa." Read into that what you will.

At Ottawa the highway splits again and becomes less relevant for the first time since leaving the east, replaced by the utilitarian Highway 401 to southern Ontario. Instead, the TCH here is a tourist road, the old route from Ottawa to Toronto or to North Bay, good for Sunday drives and antique road shows. Most commerce from the west is with Toronto, and the Trans-Canada is more of a state of mind than a means of transportation, literally sidelined by the busy 400-series highways. That's okay. There should be some romance left for an icon.

It plugs through the woods of northern Ontario, where there are three separate highways, each claiming the status of our national road: the traditional scenic route along the north shore of Lake Superior that's paralleled by the original logging route through Kapuskasing, and the southern border route that connects Thunder Bay to Rainy River, as well as the traditional route that winds beside Kenora. Here, the Trans-Canada is Everyroad, the only asphalt connection to the rest of the world.

When the woods and rocks give way to the flatland grass, the highway takes a deep breath and plunges across the prairie, running straight and wide as a cowboy belt all the way to the mountains. It's the working link that connects the west, replacing the railway in importance and general use. It splits in Manitoba and heads through both Calgary and Edmonton on its route to the ocean. People live alongside, even between — the median itself is farmed for hay.

And then, in British Columbia, it heads high over the mountains of the passes at Kicking Horse and Rogers before reverting, again, to a tourist road west of Kamloops, bypassed by the more direct Coquihalla. When the current Coke was opened in the mid-1980s, traffic on the Trans-Canada dried up as if a switch had flicked it off. Now the volume of cars on the winding road is more like the original designers expected it to be.

Finally, on Vancouver Island the highway slows into a morass of stoplight-controlled intersections — about as many as in its entire length elsewhere — on its route south to Mile 0 at Victoria. Here the road is the only route to Victoria without taking another ferry, and it crosses the mountain on the same short stretch of the Malahat Highway that was opened in 1912, when the Trans-Canada was first proposed.

So is it all that was hoped for when Albert Todd ordered a medal struck, and its creation was anticipated within the decade?

Of course it is. It's not a soulless interstate, good only for getting places fast on the superslab. Nor is it inadequate and poorly maintained, though it's frequently subpar. It has its challenges but it's overcome them in the most Canadian way possible: with lots of federal-provincial bickering, plenty of committees and discussion, and a fair amount of backroom dealing, all dragged together by normal people through the blood, sweat, and gears of superhuman physical construction to change our country for the better.

The Trans-Canada Highway is the only link in this country that we can actually touch, that connects every province and is accessible to anybody, whenever we want it. And like peace and democracy, we must be able to take it for granted — it's part of being Canadian.

Of Related Interest

Indochina Now and Then
George Fetherling
978-1-554884254
$24.99

In *Indochina Now and Then*, George Fetherling recounts multiple journeys through Vietnam, Laos, and Cambodia, keeping an eye peeled and
an ear cocked for whatever faint traces of French rule might remain.
While doing so he searches diligently in village markets, curio shops,
and rubbish bins, not to mention bookstalls along the Seine in Paris, for
early picture postcards of Southeast Asia, the sort that native Frenchmen
and Frenchwomen sent home to Europe.

The book is illustrated with 60 such images, most of them taken before
the First World War. They evoke vanished ways of life in these exotic
"lands of charm and cruelty" that have survived the wars and turmoil
of the late 20th century to emerge, smiling enigmatically, as the friendly
face of free-market socialism. In its prose and pictures, *Indochina Now
and Then* is a travel narrative that will leave an indelible impression in
the reader's imagination.

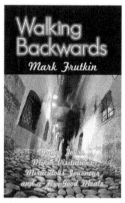

Walking Backwards
Grand Tours, Minor Visitations, Miraculous Journeys,
and a Few Good Meals
Mark Frutkin
978-1-554889327
$19.99

As travellers, we are always walking backwards, forever on the verge of step-ping into the unknown, never knowing what waits around the next corner.

You could be lost, forget your passport, fall ill. You could be served a bowl of food and not know whether it's animal, vegetable, or mineral. Even flushing the toilet can be an adventure.

You are a child again, innocent and hoping for the best, forced to trust strangers. Quite often this works out. Not always.

Walking Backwards is a return to 10 cities and what happened there. Whether inadvertently smuggling cloth into Istanbul, reading poetry in New Delhi to a crowd expecting a world-famous pianist, or wandering endlessly through Mantua searching for a non-existent hotel on a street that's fallen off the map, Mark Frutkin is a master at rediscovering the magic at the heart of all travel.

Visit us at
Dundurn.com | Definingcanada.ca | @dundurnpress | Facebook.com/dundurnpress

Printed in the USA
CPSIA information can be obtained
at www.ICGtesting.com
JSHW012034140824
68134JS00033B/3060